LGND TLK

VOL 1

The Fastest Way to a Fresh Start
(The Hustle Sold Separately)

By Marcus "Lil Keke" Edwards

All rights reserved under the international and Pan-American copyright conventions.

First published in the United States of America.

All rights reserved. With the exception of brief quotations in a review, no part of this book may be reproduced or transmitted, in any form, or by any means, electronic or mechanical (including photocopying), nor may it be stored in any information storage and retrieval system without written permission from the publisher.

DISCLAIMER

The advice contained in this material might not be suitable for everyone. The author designed the information to present his opinion about the subject matter. The reader must carefully investigate all aspects of any business decision before committing to him or herself. The author obtained the information contained herein from sources he believes to be reliable and from his own personal experience, but he neither implies nor intends any guarantee of accuracy. The author is not in the business of giving legal, accounting, or any other type of professional advice. Should the reader need such advice, he or she must seek services from a competent professional. The author particularly disclaims any liability, loss, or risk taken by individuals who directly or indirectly act on the information contained herein. The author believes the advice presented here is sound, but readers cannot hold him responsible for either the actions they take or the risk taken by individuals who directly or indirectly act on the information contained herein.

Published by Slfmade713 Publishing
Printed in the United States
Copyright © 2021 by Marcus Edwards
ISBN 978-057829641-8

DEDICATION

This book is dedicated to all of the Living Legends out here who are looking to take their lives to the next level!

TABLE OF CONTENTS

Legend Talk

Introduction 1

Chapter 1

Are you a winner? 3

Chapter 2

Moving On 11

Chapter 3

What's Your Addiction? 19

Chapter 4

Life is Very Unforgiving 25

Chapter 5

Leave it All on the Field 33

Chapter 6

Everybody Can't Go 41

Chapter 7

Instant Gratification 49

Chapter 8

Assets & Liabilities 57

Chapter 9

Both Sides of the Line 65

Chapter 10
    Keep Your Grass Cut & Sweep Your Own Porch 71

Chapter 11
    Trading Places 77

Chapter 12
    The Choice is Yours; Living or Existing 85

Chapter 13
    Self Inflicted Pain 93

Chapter 14
    Peacefully Unsatisfied 101

About the Author 109

LEGEND TALK

INTRODUCTION

Legend Talk is a way of life. It's a mindset. It's the platform that I built for not only me but for people from all walks of life that I can motivate and aspire to be the best versions of themselves. No matter your background, race, where you are from, financial status, career, or situation, it doesn't matter. You could be self-employed, in Corporate America, homeless, or part of a Fortune 500. Here's an opportunity for you to give your outlook and your random thoughts. You can give your opinions without being judged. That's Legend Talk.

Everybody is some type of coach of life because we are all going through something, or we know someone going through something. We hear about situations we would just love to get a solution for, especially from somebody who may be going through it. They may not look like us or be from the same place we are from, but that doesn't mean that they do not have the experience. Even me, sharing my life as a father, a son, a husband, and an entrepreneur for over 25 years, I never act as if I have all the answers.

So, when I built Legend Talk, it wasn't just about my attitude or the way I have seen life or perceived it; it was about day-to-day life experiences with people from all walks of life. So, when I wrote this book, one of the best feelings about it was not only that I was helping people get better, and they were helping me get better. I felt good knowing you can start this book from any chapter because it's all based on life. It's based on everyday situations from people who are just living.

It doesn't matter if you are up in the morning, fixing your coffee, getting ready for the treadmill, dropping the kids off, going home from work, or going to work.

So how can we just tap in and have a real-life conversation about making life make sense?

Welcome to Legend Talk.

CHAPTER 1

ARE YOU A WINNER?

Everybody wants to win! Win the game. Win the contest. Win the woman. Win the man. Win the money. Everyone is intrigued by the gratification, satisfaction, and feeling that come with winning. Now the flip side to it is nobody likes to lose, nobody. But in my years of experience in becoming a winner. I learned that you must find a way to accept your losses first. And that becomes easier when you figure out there is a win in every loss.

If you learn something, you picked up something in that loss; most winners know how to make that a win for them. One of the most difficult things about winning that took me years to mature was that I had to learn how to let others win. Some people are not used to winning, which brings out bitterness, hatred, envy, and jealousy when you win in a space they would like to conquer.

Sometimes, the leader in you has to find a way to create opportunities for people to be better. That's what a boss does; that's what a leader does. Put people in situations where they can make the best of themselves so that they can be winners. And sometimes, you have to know that if you are in a winning situation where you do everything you can, you are putting in time and effort for this person, this team, and this family to win. Once they finally win, that's supposed to be a win for you. But some people think winning is just the top spot. It's the person with all accolades, all the glory, the person who received all the notoriety in the situation.

Now, sometimes you can just be a part of the winning team. Do you know what I'm saying? That should make you a winner until you get your opportunity to be a winner in your own right. People are not able to determine if they're a winner or not. Because they only think winning is when all the glory and fame in the crowd and everybody stands up for you. Now, you have to determine what's a winning situation sometimes. What's a winning atmosphere? What's a winning team? That's how you become a winner; that's what I had to do.

I had to stop worrying about if the only way that I was winning was if I was coming out on top. I start helping teams win, helping people win. Clapping for others, so they can clap for me when it's my time. That's creating a winning environment. Winning is not always about you getting all the fame. Some people just don't know how to win because they can't identify what's a win for them. For example, I used to treat my life like baseball. Everybody wants to hit a home run in baseball because everyone wants to knock it out of the park. It's the best feeling the crowd standing up, everybody cheering. You go around the bases without being stopped and can score a point off the first hit, a home run.

Well, the thing about it is that it's the hardest thing to do, and everybody can't hit a home run, but that doesn't mean you can't win the game. Find a way to get the first, second, and third base and then score the point. That's a winner's mentality. I may not be able to knock it out of the park. I may not be able to hit a home run every time I go to the plate. But that doesn't mean I can't get on base and help my team win.

I may have to bunt the ball. I may have to steal a base. I may have to let four balls turn into fouls. I may have to get hit with the ball. Whatever it is to win the game. You may not always get to knock it out of the park. What will you do to win? Some people are so possessed with winning that they'll do anything to win from a cutthroat standpoint. Whether it's I have to cheat. I have to lie. I'm just addicted to winning. So, whatever it takes.

And sometimes, you can do that from a negative standpoint. So, winning is not always about what you can do better than somebody, how you can outdo somebody, and how you can have more than them. Sometimes winning is a winning smile. Seeing somebody else win is smiling because you will eventually get your turn.

Everybody and anybody can be a winner. It's just certain people can't win in things that they would like to. It's not that they can't win in anything. You just can't win in this particular thing that you want to win in. That's when sometimes it takes a collaborative effort to win. Stop missing out on your wins because you can't lead the charge. Somebody else might have a great idea. Somebody else might have the finances to put in play. Somebody else might lead the situation, but you are alone for the ride to get the win. Get used to winning, see the formula, and make yourself bigger.

It's not that you can't win in everything that you want; learn how to make it a collaborative effort sometimes. Learn how to win in silence; the two go together; it's kind of getting used to winning. We don't have to tell people our plays because we're on the same team. Do you get what I'm saying? Some people can't win without telling. You have to learn how to win; I had to learn how to win when learning when to listen instead of talking. That's winning. Learn when to sit in the back of the room and let the people in the front get to win because this is the thing.

Winning isn't fun by yourself, but you have to surround yourself with people who know how to win and people who are used to winning. That's going to be the fastest way for you to become a winner because let me tell you something. Losing is contagious. It's bad energy. It's a bad vibe. And that's what I found out. Hanging around losers', you start making it normal. Mediocracy drowning in your sorrows they depressed is always negative. Next thing you know, you got sympathy for that, sorrow. See, I call that living under a black cloud, waiting on something bad to happen.

I'm not telling you that life is not full of challenges. I'm just saying; that it's people who expect it; they are waiting on it. That is contagious. Do you know what their motto is? I can't win for losing. See, you can also speak in existence; you can speak up in existence, fear, doubt. Negative vibes

come from all types of actions speaking on it. See, I used to figure out ways, and a good thing I picked up in winning was finding out how to get other people credit for my wins. You know, making them feel just as great. It was us.

You don't always have to stand at the front. It's people that let people get all the highlights, get all the fame, and they stood in the back, and they still were just as big as a winner or won just as y accolades as the other people, but they won in silence. Sometimes, even in relationships. You know, this isn't the most attractive woman. She's not the smartest, but she works hard. She has your best interest. She gets it. I'm not telling you to settle, but this you may love has so much going on. Her appearance is better. Her shape is better. She's part of the in-crowd, but she could never love you. She'll never make you number one.

I'm not telling you don't shoot for the moon and stars. I'm saying sometimes identify what's the win for you, and winning maybe you such a winner. This woman right here, you may be able to turn her into a winner. You may be able to do something and raise her game. That's the sign of a winner. The same goes for women on this topic. He works hard, brings home the check, and takes care of the bills; he does what he needs to do. I'm not telling you to settle, but this big old that's strong. He got all the money, got the fancy cars. He'll start in the streets, never love you or never have time for you, and never marry you.

Identify what's a win for you. Winning is not always about settling, which makes you a loser because you're in a losing situation. It's called making the best out of your situation, and great winners turn their situations into winning situations. Is winning everything the only thing is winning a thing. Well, I'll tell you this, winning is a great thing, depending on how you look at life. It doesn't make you a loser because you don't see winning the same way I do. That's why it goes back to what's a win for you? Hey, you got people, who have been homeless, who lost their families. And, this 9 to 5 job, this nice Honda, this nice Ford truck is a win for me. Do you know what I'm saying?

This portion of this three-story home and these jewels and this jewelry might be a win for you, but where I'm coming from; this is a win for me. That's what the thing for me. Sometimes, I wasn't platinum, I wasn't gold, but God bless me to be alive and free. God blessed me with a situation where I didn't have to answer anybody because I could make my own decisions. I wouldn't always be where I wanted to be, but I was in situations where I could win and keep winning. I won't be worried about no more ten years down the line, where Imma be in 7 years or eight years. How can I get this win in the next month? That will lead to me being a winner in the next six months. That will lead me to be a winner in the next year—a short-term goal.

Like I said in the beginning. Identify what's a win for you; whether it's you leading the charge, you being a part of a winning situation, become a winner, and it leads back to the main question, are you a winner?

You got to stop creating doubt. Winning is confidence. If you are going into something already, not thinking you can do it or get it done. You already lost. You are speaking things into existence. People be saying that's corny. Or that's just some people say, no, well not for me because everything with me is about my faith. You believe without sin. Faith, so you have to things into existence. Sometimes when you want to become a winner in your role to become successful, you got to make realistic expectations. So, you can be a winner.

Set some short-term goals. Things that I can get done. I can see the forest for the trees. It's in my reach. I used to tell my son when he was going to college, getting ready for college, and putting his degree plan together—Y'all making this 5, 6-year degree plan which is fine. Shoot for the stars, but your year into it, your first six months into it, you start having a bumpy roll with it. It isn't going the way you want it to. Now you start telling yourself, 'I can't even see five years from now. I can't get done now.'

Well, you need to make short-term goals; how can I knock this next semester down? How can I just get this one class together? How can I just finish this first year, wrap this up and then go in the next year? Short-term goals, where you can make yourself a winner faster. Instead of creating a situation that leads to a losing environment, you feel like I'm a loser. That's why I ask, 'Are you a winner?' And finding out what kind of winner you are is everything. Because you got some people that will do anything to win, Cutthroat, lie, cheat, steal, you have to watch them. Because winning can bring out the best in you, and it can bring out the worst in you.

It's all about what type of winner you are and what type of winning mentality you got? When you hate losing, you do anything to win. But it's a thin line between winning and losing. Yeah, that's for sure. And I used to have a problem with one of the main things you got to have to be a winner. I used to have; it was my biggest problem. Finishing. Procrastination is the first sign of losing. Find out how to close out. Find out how to finish whatever it is the task, the job, the to-do list, the goal list.

The glory and the feeling that comes with having a to-do list or a goal list with ten things on them, and you did create and finished 8, with two more to go, that start creating a winning vibe. Because that's what winning is. Winning is energy, and that's why you have to watch the negative spirits you are around. Do you know what I'm saying? Like three negative spirits and a winner that doesn't mix. Because now the bitterness and the excuses and the sorrow that come in that type of environment right there, it comes with a lot of having sympathy.

Sympathy is not the trait of a winner. I found that out the hard way. See, a couple of wins don't make you a winner. The arrogance in people will make them do this here. They'll jump off the winning train. I've had people, friends, and coworkers around me and couldn't play my part. The whole time, I crash the whole ship if I can't be the captain. , identify what's a winning situation sometimes.

One of the first assets of a winner is a winning smile. It shows confidence. See one thing about a confident person; their attitude and aura display that. They already think they can do whatever they think they're getting ready to do. It's halfway already done. You shoot out vibes to people that I got supreme control over what I'm about to do. You can't talk me out of my price because

you can't make me believe otherwise. I am in control of achieving this dream. I am in control of making this happen. That's a winning smile.

You can start with a winning smile. That's your attitude; that's how people perceive you. That's how people want to, people want to help winners, and it starts with having a winner's arrogance. So, that's the whole thing. Am I a winner? It's all about what you think a winner is and what you go about to be a winner. If being a winner is important to you and the process that goes with winning. Being able to lose, helping other people win, letting other people win, making winners of people who didn't think they knew how to win. Those are all the things about being a winner. So, are you a winner?

CHAPTER 2

MOVING ON

Moving on is a very important part of life, but for me, when it came to moving on, I feel like I learned everything the hard way. When to move on, moving on too fast, not moving on fast enough, and maybe the hardest one for me was how to move on. I've been stuck in a lot of situations. I know a lot of people who can't get past certain things and get to certain places that they should have been already but just didn't know how to move on.

You can be too stubborn; it could be fear. A lot of people don't move on based on being comfortable, and I've been through situations where we just couldn't move on based on embarrassment. I think one of the things that finally helped me in moving on was figuring out that I'm putting in all this time, all this effort, hesitant, scared, and don't know how to move on from something that'll move on for me in the blink of an eye. That's when I started determining and started coming up with a better outlook on how to move on because I started asking myself. This same thing that's killing me or got me procrastinating about moving on from it, if I put it in the same situation, vice versa, switched the roles, how fast could it move on from me? Whether that was a person, a business deal, or a bad habit, whatever it is, how long would it take this thing to move on from me? Moving on is not always from a relationship, bad friendship, or moving on from a bad business deal. Sometimes you have to move on from an argument.

It's people who get glory and satisfaction out of going against the grain. They can know you're right; they can understand everything you're saying but getting under your skin is a better thing to do at the time. Sometimes, as a person, when you mature, you got to learn when to leave well enough alone. You can't beat a dead horse. You already know the stop sign is red, but you will sit here and argue for 30 minutes that it's blue. Sometimes, you have to move on from the argument; move on from the conversation.

Everybody knows that it takes two people to argue. And I used to love the debate. Until I realized that the people I was going back and forth with never intended to see the truth out of the situation; it was more about not giving me the props or not giving me the satisfaction of making me think that I was right about something. Those were the times when I just had to figure out that sometimes you have to move on from things that don't even make sense. You got to move on instead of waddling in a situation that ain't going to get no better no matter how long you talk about it.

You know, not only me, but I know a lot of people who couldn't move on from relationships just based on comfort. "For instance, I have no idea how to step out on faith. I have no idea how to believe in myself. So, this person controls my self-esteem. They control my financial situation. They control my mindset, and I'm in a terrible situation. They could be a person that I'm not happy with ever. Nothing is going right, but "I'm comfortable." That's the first sign of not knowing how to move on. Never let anybody hold you, hostage in an unfair or unhealthy situation just because they figured out you don't know how to move on. I know men and I have partners who came home from jail, and they've lost everything; that's a much better situation for them to get out on their own, but they don't have anything. They don't have a home, a cooked meal, or active employment yet, so they are in situations where they may not be happy. They may not be getting treated right in the household where they're staying, but they just have no way to move on.

Sometimes, you have to let all that go and just step out with God; step out on faith because not moving on will put both of y'all in a situation where eventually it's going to become toxic enough where either you are going to explode. You'll never be able to fix or rekindle the situation you are in, or you are going to sit there and rot and become bitter and unhappy, ungrateful, unsatisfied, and unappreciative in the situation that you just couldn't move on from.

There are going to be situations where you grew up with people all your life. Little league football, church, spending the night at each other house, graduating from school, middle school, high school, getting ready for college, going to the club, hanging out on the corner. Whatever it is, we did everything together, but at 30 or 40, in some way, we've outgrown each other, and where your maturity level and my maturity level might not be at the same level. And that can cause or bring about a time when we must move on.

People don't understand that I had to do it for myself; it wasn't always about whether I was right or if I out matured somebody and needed to move on from them. You know what, I started seeing, as a person, you have to realize when you need to remove yourself from somebody else life. Where they harvest, where they go, and what their blessing is just not mixing with what you're doing. You may be in a time in your life when things are not going right, and things aren't in place. You are still getting yourself together; you got to get yourself together to do what you need to do. And you may need to move on from that person to give them a chance to be great.

It's not always on your side. Know when to move on yourself—not moving on because you need to remove this person from your life, but sometimes you have to move on to give other people an opportunity to be great in their space. But, sometimes, you can move on too fast. Some people are not patient enough. They are in a rush, and they're in a hurry to get to the next best thing. And something that you should've grown with and that could've been a blessing to you; you just didn't have the patience for it. You know what I'm saying?

Many people move on quickly to what looks good in the public eye or what looks great to the people, but that might not have been a win for you, and it might not be time for you to move on. But a lot of people move on too fast. You know what I'm saying? I've been in that situation myself.

One of the craziest things, too, is moving on from family. Yeah, it happens! It can come a time when you got to move on from your mother, father, sister, brother, and cousin. And when I say moving on, I'm saying that sometimes you have to love people from afar.

You know people, not all the time your siblings or family members are blessed with the same hustle you got, the same attitude, the same mindset you got. You know what I'm saying? And you can be a person that wants to help your family member as much as you can; you can want to see them in the same capacity as you, having great things or living life, but sometimes, you know you have to move on from family members that it just couldn't work. It just couldn't happen. And it is family members who don't want to see you happy if they are not happy, or don't want to see you with it if they don't have it, just like a stranger. That's when you have to make a tough and difficult decision; sometimes, you have to move on from your family.

You know, like generational curses and things that have been passed down. You can either stay there living in it or try to move on from that situation. And that's tough, moving on from family because some people can't make that decision. You know what I'm saying? And what would you rather do; lose everything you got, trying to make sure that your cousin or your uncle has the same amount you have? Again, it comes a time when you have to move on.

It's people who go to work seven days a week, 12 hours a day. They can't have an opinion at their job. They can't ever be late, can't prosper, can't flourish, and don't know how to move on. But the flip side is they can be fired or replaced, and the job can move on from them anytime. Sometimes you must step up, believe in yourself, and just move on. Pick what's best for you. You can't always pick what's best for the next person. You know what I'm saying? What's going to make them happy? Some have the attitude of "you know I'm gonna continue to do a good job and show up on time because it's the best that works out for them."

Sometimes you have to pick yourself, which starts with knowing when to move on and can be a part of not moving on fast enough. It's people who will just stay on the ship until it sinks. That comes like; sometimes, you can invest; it can be your family; your friends; it can just be an investment for yourself, and it just didn't work out the way it was supposed to, but you have to know when to move on.

Don't lose your house, don't lose your family by trying to stick it out and see something that just didn't work. It could be a time where "hey, man, I may be about to move on too fast, but then it can be, "I'm not moving on fast enough," and you're about to carry out a situation that has no life in it. There is no win in it. But you couldn't identify or figure out when to move on.

I remember owning my own Little League football team.

During that time, I coached a lot of seasons, and I got an opportunity to coach my 9-year-old. One of the moving-on lessons that I used to teach him was moving on from bad plays and good plays. Stop being stuck with your mistake because you missed an assignment, the tackle, or you didn't catch the ball. Life moves on so fast; the game moves on so fast; the more you dwell on that mistake, the next play is happening so fast; you can't get your mind wrapped around what's happening right now.

The same thing applies to good plays. Don't get wrapped up in that when you score a touchdown, catch the ball, or make a good tackle. Move on because it's bigger and better, and more things will happen in the game. I start applying that to business. You know what I'm saying? If I made a bad investment or decided to do something that didn't work out, I just had to figure out how to move on. The same happens when I make a good investment or put my money into something, and it happens as fast as I thought. I had to learn how to move on from that because it could be bigger, better things. It could be another challenge, something greater than I can get to, but you have to have the mindset of knowing when to move on, whether good or bad.

So, that's what I used to tell him: bad play, good play. Figure out a way to move on because that's how fast life and that's how fast the game is moving. And to close out, one thing you must understand is that sometimes you have to move on to prosper. Sometimes you have to move on to grow. Sometimes, you have to move on to reach better heights. You know what I'm saying? You are not always moving on because it's a negative outcome that will come with it. Sometimes to get better and reach your full potential, you have to know how to move on.

And one of the hardest ones that I think we all struggle with is understanding that life moves on.

Do you know what an OG told me? You wouldn't be, or nobody wouldn't be so wrapped up in impressing people and showing them everything they got if they knew how fast people moved on when they died. And that was something that I started to study and understand. I call it the "it doesn't stop." People can die Wednesday; Thursday night, people are still going to have a drink. Friday, people are still going to celebrate their anniversary. On Sunday, people will still sit down, watch football, and eat barbecue. Life doesn't stop. I'm not telling you that people don't mourn, people don't grieve, and that people don't have feelings. I'm just telling you that the difference between grieving and moving on is a thin line. People have to understand that life goes on. And sometimes, as hard as it is and as sad as it is, you have to respect the fact that people move on.

People die on Mondays; people resume work on Friday, on Tuesday to be exact. So, moving on is always thought of as something I had to get away from this person. I had to move on from this relationship. I'm tired.

Now, moving on can be so many elements. I am moving on from the relationship, moving on from the argument, moving on from the business deal, and moving on in life because you understand that life moves on. So, I just want to do a great chapter about moving on because I think it plays a very significant part in everybody's life. I am moving on.

CHAPTER 3

WHAT'S YOUR ADDICTION?

See, every time we hear the word addicted or addiction, we think it's drug-related. We think about crack, cocaine, weed, and anything related to drugs. When the truth is, we are all addicted to something.

People are addicted to power, addicted to control. Some people are addicted to money, addicted to sex, complaining; love; sympathy, you name it. It starts with understanding what addiction is. One of the first things you must do is, figure out how long it will take you before you determine that this is not a bad habit; it's an addiction.

People sometimes think, "man, I just got a bad habit; I do this a little too much. I can stop." Nah, it has turned into an addiction. Something you're mentally or physically dependent on. It can be a substance, an activity, or a thing. Something that eventually you can't control is not a habit; it's an addiction. You don't have to look at it as a drug, but sometimes it has the same effect as a drug. You can be addicted and lose self-respect; you know you can be addicted to power and begin losing friends, losing dignity.

Yes, you can experience the same effects as being addicted to drugs, but drugs aren't the only thing you can be addicted to.

How long does it take to determine this is not a bad habit; it is an addiction?

What habit do you have that you repeatedly do, you repeatedly tell yourself you're in control of, but you can't stop doing it? People don't like to admit or claim the word addiction because it's related to the failure. It's related to not being in control, but at the end of the day, you're addicted.

A lot of people are addicted to control. You know, "I'm buying the food, picking the restaurant; I pay the bills, I'm going to run the house. Well, the thing about it is that sometimes that control is given to people you're around who are inferior to you. They empower you with this power. They may not have as much money to buy the food or pick the restaurant; they might not have the self-esteem to tell you when you're wrong; so they continue to laugh at every joke, and they continue to praise all of the things they may know are wrong, but they're afraid to tell you. They continue to make you seem right in many situations that you may be wrong in. You can become addicted to that control. You can become addicted to that power because you're not surrounded by enough people telling you that that isn't it. And you take that control to your job, into other friendships and business.

People are addicted. Sometimes people can be very disrespectful, real disregarding, and overwhelming, and they do it so long; they say, "I got a bad habit of helping people, or I got a bad habit of talking." No, they're addicted to controlling the narrative.

For some people, the only way they can see it is if you see it their way. They're the smartest in the room; their accolades and paperwork make them believe you should see it their way because you're not qualified to see it based on their standards. They're egotistical and addicted to power.

Control isn't always a dictatorship where you must tell somebody what to do. Sometimes it's controlling the narrative, the mindset, and the room from a negative standpoint. Addicted.

What's your addiction?

People love to say; I'm addicted to money. Yeah, man, I'm a hustler. I'm addicted to getting money. You know that doesn't always have to be a positive thing. You could be addicted to getting money just out of reach and out of touch with everything else.

You're so addicted to getting money that you're not paying attention to your health and get a tumor the size of a grapefruit growing inside your body? What about being so addicted to getting money that your spouse, loved one, your husband, or your wife has an affair in the house that you're living in, but you never pay attention because you're addicted to money. You've looked over all the small things in life.

Everything that's not related to getting money. Yeah, that could be to your detriment, sometimes being addicted to getting money. It's not always a great thing.

What is your addiction, and what are the positive and negative outcomes of having an addiction?

We are all addicted to something. You could be addicted to being nice. You could be addicted to being respectful. I'm not saying all addictions are one, but what I'm saying is that we all have them. And sometimes they can either lead us to go too far into that addiction, not realizing that I'm addicted to something that I can't control, that may be hindering my success, stopping me from moving on. It may be hurting other people... An addiction is something that we do not have control over. Mentally or physically dependent on this particular thing.

People are mentally and physically dependent on love. You can be just addicted to love. Addicted to the out of it and addicted to the emotions of it. Addicted to the phrase, I love you. That's how some people are in love with 2 or 3 people at one time because they are just addicted to the feeling and the emotion that comes with the word love. "I can't live without it. I can't control it".

Being addicted to love can also have you addicted to sympathy. You love pats on the back. You can't do anything without somebody telling you that you did good and look good. You love attention, the accolades and glory that come with compliments.

People can become addicted to complaining. See that bad habit you have of always finding a negative in everything. That bad habit you got of always trying to figure out how it isn't going to work. The reason it all went bad. See that becomes an addictive format of complaining. That's all you do is complain. It's contagious. It's very bad energy you can give out, and people start being attached to complaining.

Find a way for something to be wrong in every situation; people live like that, just like we said, addicted to attention. Just addicted to "it's nothing that I can do where I don't want people to see it or have something positive to say to me. Congratulate me in some way. I need somebody to clap for me all the time." It's people who are addicted to that feeling. They don't know how to feel self-gratification. They don't know how to make themselves, do something for themselves. And it's just enough that they got it done in their mind frame. They need somebody to tell them it was good. It was great.

You got people who love to fight at the club. I love to fight at the party so that somebody can break it up. The attention that goes with getting the fight broke up; I love it.' They are addicted to it.

What are you addicted to? I had to realize that I had an addictive personality. An addictive personality is when you are addicted to more things than one at a time. I had an addictive personality to power, control, sex, all of them. Because once you reach a certain amount of success, a certain level of success in your life tends to bring an ego. You know, an ego of loving things going your way. You get used to things going your way, which can become very addictive.

I found myself being addicted to revenge, addicted to getting back, which will always have you in a situation where you are always trying to prove something. Whether that's proving something to somebody else, proving something to the crowd, or proving something to yourself. Revenge has you always trying to prove something, which can become very addictive.

I was addicted to things like that until I figured out what I could do to rid myself of the addictive personality. I had to conclude that we are all addicted to something; what can I do? And one of the main things I started trying was mixing it. I may be addicted to certain things, but I try to mix it with a good habit to offset it; I'm addicted to winning. Whether it's the card game, debate, or whatever it was. Getting to the money, I was addicted to winning.

So, a good habit that I tried to pick up was becoming a person with a good habit having a great habit of helping other people win. No matter how much I like to win, a better habit I was gaining and trying to master was, helping other people win. And I think that's a great way to offset addiction. You are addicted to power. You are addicted to control. Form a great habit of giving. Form a great habit of compromise. You are addicted to running the show. You may be addicted to being a boss or in control. Well, make a great habit of trying to have self-control. Be addicted to respect, not just that you want to get for yourself but be addicted to giving others respect. So, that was my way of trying to offset my addictions, finding great habits to mix with them.

Addiction is mentally or physically dependent on a person, a thing, or an activity, and we're all addicted to something. Sit yourself down sometime and look at your bad habits and see how far they've gotten out of control and led you to do something you think you're in control of but are not. But at the same time, people feel like they can break a bad habit whenever they want to. But a bad habit that has turned into addiction is much stronger than you think.

We must not be afraid of communicating and seeking help through therapy. Don't be so afraid to speak to somebody who specializes in an addiction that you may have.

One of the first things to do is step up and not be afraid to say, "I'm addicted to such and such." And some of the harder ones in life are sex addiction, love, and fame. Don't be scared to talk about things that have gotten out of control. That's what I had to do. I had to stop being so scared of therapy, stop being afraid to communicate, and admit to myself that I had an addiction.

What's your addiction?

CHAPTER 4

LIFE IS VERY UNFORGIVING

Life can be very unforgiving. There are certain things that people are going to hold against you that they will never let go of. No matter how much time has passed; how much you've asked them for forgiveness; no matter how long the healing process has gone by, they will never let it go.

And I'm saying that because there are people still caught up with the mindset that allows them to give power to what other people think of them based on past actions. To combat this, you have to learn how to forgive yourself. See. Eventually, you must ask God for forgiveness and be strong enough to forgive yourself.

I've been in situations where people can see your growth; you're doing better for yourself; you can see you prospering and changing, no longer the person you used to be. But, based on where they are in their life, their happiness, and where they want to be, they will hold a specific thing against you because they like to see you suffer from it. They don't want to get past it. Everyone else is praising the new person you've become, but for this person, they hold on to what you did that may have hurt them and want you to stay in the hurt with them. It happens.

In a situation like this, you must learn to forgive yourself, move on, and successfully live in the past. Successfully living in the past is where you are doing good in life, things are going great for you, and God is blessing you in many ways. It's your harvest, your season, but you still hold on to that grudge. You still want revenge when they embarrassed or humiliated you or didn't go the way you were supposed to when it wasn't going your way. You're successful, growing, and prospering in all types of new ventures in your life, but you are still holding on to that ill will inside you from when it wasn't going your way. That's called successfully living in the past. See, people do that all the time.

Your past can either help you or hurt you. When people notice that you are having a hard time getting past your past, you're shuffling in it; you're stuck in that situation, you can't move past it; they'll continue to remind you of it. It is up to you to be strong enough to understand that you've outgrown the person you used to be. That you're not going to continue to let who you were in your 20s control who you are in your 30s. But it's people that will continue to remind you of your past as long as they can see that you cannot get past it.

People don't always want physical revenge or physical get back. It can be mental. They'll "pray it" on you in some cases, but most people believe in karma much more than you think. Because people believe in you got what's coming to you going to get what's yours all that. With that being said, you must learn how to forgive yourself because there are going to be people who aren't going to ever forgive you.

Life is very unforgiving. Even with myself, one of my hardest things to do about forgiving was based on what you did to me, when you did it to me and how I was doing in life at the time.

For example, if I called you in a time of need, down on some finances, and I shared my tough time with you confidently or confided in you somehow. And then I heard it from somebody else in a joking manner or in a way that you were making a derogatory point about where I'm at in life. It used to be hard for me; maybe I'll forget, but it used to be hard for me to forgive based on how I was doing. Did you kick me when I was down?

Because I struggled with thinking that being cordial was forgiveness, we still speak, and I'm able to shake your hand, but I don't trust you anymore. I don't want a close business or friendship with you anymore. The truth is, I haven't forgiven you; being cordial is not forgiving. I came to terms with the only person that was getting hurt or still being affected by it was me because you might be dealing with a person that has forgiven their self.

So, if they've forgiven themselves and moved on, you are the only one still affected by the situation.

Life can be very unforgiving even when you're wrong. People will have the audacity to be mad at you for what they did. They couldn't find it within themselves to forgive and become mad that you moved on.

Why is it so hard for us to apologize when people are caught up in their egos? And when I say us, that's women and men; it doesn't matter. People will be mad at you for something they did because they couldn't figure out how to forgive themselves. If you forgive yourself, you can apologize without worrying about whether the person will accept it back. But people don't know how to forgive on both sides of it. Forgive and let go or forgive themselves for being able to move on in the situation better. Yeah, it goes both ways.

I've seen times in life when people have suffered from generational curses, and their upbringing sends you down a road that you weren't prepared for, making people unforgiving to their parents and families.

You can have people who have great families. They became great mothers and great fathers, and they never forgive their parents just for what they took them to and what they had to do to get there. It could've started years before their parents could have been taught wrong. Life is very unforgiving.

In relationships, it goes both ways where men have committed infidelity, cheated on a woman, slept outside of the relationship had to get a divorce. However, they may become faithful and ready to marry in the next relationship. It's people that are very unforgiving. Women are very unforgiving to that situation, where they don't think you need to be happy anymore. Based on what you did to them, how you ruined their life, and how you just cheated on them constantly, they don't think you should ever get married and have a great relationship. Very unforgiving.

The same goes for men; they feel like there's no way you cheated on me. You had two-three other men, and when you got money from other men. Now you want to settle down, get married, have a kid, and be a great housewife. Some men are very unforgiving of that. You are successfully living in the past.

I'm talking about making all kinds of money. All types of things are going your way but still holding grudges. I'm still holding on to this anger in my heart. "Ke, what's the answer to that?" I don't know. Besides, the only person that's completely damaged or still going through it is the person that still hasn't come to terms with it; I got to forgive and let go—a very hard thing to do.

CHAPTER 4: LIFE IS VERY UNFORGIVING

One of the craziest things you could be doing is having a grudge against somebody that is not even entertaining the fact that you are even mad or that you even have this particular thing against them. That will lead you to forgive yourself—sometimes, forgiving that person. Sometimes you must forgive people with hot happen to acknowledge them; every conversation is about forgiveness and letting things go. It may not be a conversation. It may be mental. You may have to do something for yourself so that you won't be dragging yourself to the mud with it for the rest of your life.

Then some people always want to know the fastest way to forgive somebody—understanding that we all need to be forgiven for something. But I don't understand how to forgive murder yet. It's a slippery slow. Maybe somebody can help me. I don't understand how to forgive rape. You have to stand in front of that before you can tell somebody how to move on in that situation. I know that it has to be done. On one side of the term, either the person had to forgive, or you have to forgive yourself to move on, or it'll be something that'll be a burden to you for the rest of your life. Life is very unforgiving.

Life can be very unforgiving. That's why you have to try to continue to evolve. And keep up with time because it's going to be accomplishments that you do, things that you have conquered in your life, and things that you have done great in the past that people are no longer going to applaud you for it. People are no longer going to recognize you for it. Life is very unforgiving. Things you worked for your whole life. Things that meant something to you, whether you feel like you are OG, whether you feel like you are a student of that particular game, whether you feel like that's become one of your best expertise. Some people are going to be very unforgiving of that. What have you done for me lately? People who moved on from who you used to be and don't respect you as the same as they probably respected you ten years ago. That's why sometimes you have to keep on evolving. Life is unforgiving like that.

You would think they'd show me some respect for the groundwork I laid or give me the proper props I deserve for putting this down years ago. It's people who move along with that, these young cats, new people, whether it is a new breed of independent women. Life is very unforgiving. People move on.

See, people think that to whom as much is given, much is required is always based on money. Sometimes, it's based on forgiveness. Sometimes, since you earn being the bigger person, you have to be the bigger person. Humble yourself. Have enough humility to know that you've made it to a level of maturity, or you've made it to a different space where you have to be forgiving on both sides.

Forgive yourself for the things that you didn't know. Forgive yourself for the things that you didn't take the time to learn when you were younger. Forgive yourself for not understanding the power of the tongue, saying something you were not supposed to say; forgive yourself for not being faithful in a relationship at a point in your life. That means forgiving yourself for breaking somebody's heart. You have to be the bigger person sometime, and because one thing about it, one of the resolutions that I came up with to help me be more forgiving is that God specializes in fresh starts. You always get an opportunity for a fresh start if you are really about making change.

Some people think fresh starts are moving out of a house, getting a new place, or getting rid of an old car note, and now you got a new car.

Nah, a fresh start on a change in life, a new beginning. A fresh start on putting some old things, some old addictions, and things I didn't move on from to become a winner. Now that doesn't mean you've grown just because you are successful. Success doesn't always make you outgrow something; that's why I say it is successfully living in the past; that was in the beginning, but learning how to forgive in either situation that you are in; from the person that needs to get the forgiveness, and sometimes you got to be the person that gives the forgiveness. Unforgiven.

CHAPTER 5

LEAVE IT ALL ON THE FIELD

There is no tomorrow. One of my greatest accomplishments was figuring out how to mentally stop putting off today for tomorrow, not physically. See, you can need to wash the dishes, take the trash out, and cut the yard, and you may have time for that tomorrow, but you physically can get that done today. What about mentally not putting off today things you have to put your mind to, things you have to study for, goals that you had to write down and work for. It's a lot of times we put off today for tomorrow in that aspect, and many people live in regret because you can have what it takes to be a winner. You don't know how to finish, and you don't know how to close out. Unfinished business and unfinished opportunities result from not leaving it all on the field.

Give it all you got the first time. That way, you can walk away with your head high; no matter if you lose or win, you are good with the result because you took advantage of every opportunity. Your first impression was your last impression.

Sometimes, play the game hard as if there's not going to be another game. Some people complain with way less. They couldn't wait for this opportunity to step out on the field. I'm using the field as an analogy, but leave it all on the field at the job, in this relationship, in this career move. No stones unturned. You have to understand that, for the most part, people are going to do what they love; people are going to do what they are addicted to; that's what's going to be most important to them. And I found that you will give everything you got for what's important to you or find an excuse.

People do not get talked out of anything they love because they aren't going to tell it. That's what I used to do anything I want to get done, and I feel like it's going to be some backlash, or it's going to be some hate, or it's going to be some people going against what I'm saying, and I want to do it then I don't tell. That's what I do.

If we knew how much time we had to live and how close we were to getting to our happiness or a goal, we would have stopped procrastinating. You would have been left all on the field; you would have been giving everything you got. But people think they have so much time. You don't. I don't. We don't.

Faith and hustle are action words for me. You can't be your own worst enemy, and that's what a lot of us are. Check your to-do list, and check your life list, period. Do you have more give-ups than completions? How many things have you told yourself or things that you put in your head to do that you completed? And you might be like, "I ain't getting that done." Now ask yourself how many of the same things I gave up on? Giving up is way easier than completing something.

Hard work is going to beat talent every time. Consistency is going to beat potential every time. "Finna," that word needs to be taken out of your vocabulary.

CHAPTER 5: LEAVE IT ALL ON THE FIELD

"Finna. Can't." These are the words of not leaving every stone unturned, not leaving it all on the field. There is no tomorrow. Some people have all the skills and the knowledge to get something done, but you aren't hungry for it. And you can have a person that has way fewer smarts, way less skill than you have to get something done, but they are hungry for it. Their ambition is much bigger than yours. They are going to get there before you.

When you're a person who comes from nothing, you either complain about everything or make something happen with anything. A person with drive, courage, and ambition is much more dangerous than a person that's supposedly so smart. That's when you compare street smarts and common sense; if you can get a good mixture of those, you're a dangerous person. But you have people who have all the talent. They got all the skills and training, but they have no drive.

This one meeting might be the last one. This gig might be the last one. This interview might be the last one. No tomorrow.

I had to start doing that in everything that I did. When I make this album, this might be my last album. I'm grateful, I'm blessed for every opportunity God has given me, but this might be the last one. I'm giving it all I got; this concert might be the last one. This radio concert may be the last; whether it's a podcast interview, magazine interview, or conversation, I give it all I have.

I'm real big on God going to bless your effort. I'm giving everything that I got this time. People will say, "you're living on the edge"; no, I'm leaving it all on the field.

You have to be passionate about something. It got to be something that inspires you and inspires you. See, for me, I started looking for things that motivated me that weren't money motivated. I started asking myself, "is it anything I'm dedicated to that I don't make a profit from?" And I'mma start finding ways to leave it on the field that way. For example, when you help one of your friends, don't tell your other friends. When you give advice or your opinion, keep it between you all. Do things wholeheartedly. No expectation when you give. If you loan something and it comes back, great! If it do it do; if it don't it don't. But remember, you did it as a friend; you were loyal to whatever they asked you for. That's called leaving it on the field.

People will trick you out of your spot fast. One of the fastest ways to get a trick out of your spot is by a person who can see that they want that position worse than you do. They are willing to outwork you and out grind you, out-hustle you. Whatever it is because they can see your lack of ambition. They know that you're waiting on your backing; you're waiting on your help. You're not leaving it all on the field, and some people are hungry enough to notice that in you, and they'll trick you right out of your spot.

Some people are just born with lazy genetics. The background, environment, and family you come from are just lazy. And sometimes the best advice for that is to try to surround yourself with people who want more. That doesn't mean you can't have it, or it has to be you, but you have to be smart enough and have enough drive to surrounding yourself with people who want more than you do. Because sometimes, the lack of effort and laziness can come from your family. It can come from your surroundings. Something that you've just been looking at and watching for so long. *You've become accustomed to remaining the same* person. Some people are waiting in the background for just that one shot. Call them the backup quarterback. The back quarterback is always the best person on the field. Everybody is always looking for something better; meanwhile, people are not just sitting there, you know, sitting cold. They are waiting to get that opportunity and never turn back. That's because you didn't leave it all on the field.

I'm not telling anyone to stay in anything that makes them uncomfortable. Sometimes you've been to therapy, you've been to counseling, you've had multiple conversations about how to make this marriage work; you've left it all on the field. It just didn't work out. But at least you did everything you can do so you can feel good about the effort or whatever you put into it. You left it all on the field. It just didn't work out.

Sometimes second chances from God. Whatever it may be, it is your opportunity to leave it all on the field. You may go to the doctor and learn you have a disease, an ailment. Whatever it is, it could be cancer; it could be anything. But you've been given a list of instructions to live. How to exercise, how to eat, what medicines to take, and what medicines not to take. But you didn't leave it all on the field. You are far from giving up; you're so far from thinking it's over. You could've saved your own life by doing everything you had to do to live. Left it all on the field.

'If I die tomorrow or next week, I know I took every precaution to ensure I lived in the best health. I ate what I was supposed to eat. I cleaned my life up. I left it all on the field to live.' You have to leave it all on the field for your own life. This analogy is based on giving everything you got when given opportunities; because there may be no tomorrow.

So, not only is this about not giving up, not only about being dedicated, this is mostly about not putting off today for tomorrow.

And lastly, for me, sometimes you have to leave it all on the field with your friends, family, brother, and coworker. Tell them you love them now. Give them their flowers today. Support their business today. Please show your appreciation and gratitude and how grateful you are to have them in your life today. Leave it all on the field. Life is very, very short. A process of leaving it all on the field sometimes you have to do that from a physical standpoint and mental standpoint but praise your people now. Have that father-son moment now. Have that mother-daughter moment now. Don't keep putting it off. Have a family reunion now.

Take that family trip and see your grandmother or your grandfather that's on their last days. Do that now. Leave no stone unturned. Leave it all on the field. Don't go to the funeral with regrets about what I should've done last year, six months. Fix it with your, fix it with Aunt Sarah now. Fix it with Uncle Charles today. Fix it with your mama now. If you can, if you got that opportunity. Leave it all on the field.

The older I got, the humbler I became, and the more grateful I got. When I start coming to terms that no one owes me anything. Any advice, help, anything that anybody gives is always a blessing. So, leaving it all on the field meant being mature enough to understand that these opportunities are foreign in anything, not just in life, business, relationships, and just living. How can I be more dedicated to getting it done the first chance I got to do it? How can I wrap my mind around that I may not get another chance to make this go right? I may not get another chance to fix the wrong I got with somebody. I might not get another opportunity to grow in this particular thing. Please take advantage of it now. That's the point. Take advantage of your opportunities, and in the space, God has given you, do it while you can. Not living under regret; finishing. That's what it's about. Leaving it all on the field.

CHAPTER 6

EVERYBODY CAN'T GO

Everybody can't go. Sometimes you must stop trying to take people to the top with you who don't even want to see you there. You have aspirations of building something so great, and you go up the ladder and reach the top and bring these people with you, but they don't want to see you at the top. You have to learn to let people go and leave certain people where they are, or you will get left there with them. That's how life works out sometime. You have to leave certain people where they are or stay there with them.

The way your heart beats, your hustle, and your mindset is set up is not set up the same way for them. And you are steady, sharing, and trying to get them to see your dream, and they'll never have the same motivation or inspiration you have to pour into you or provide any form of support.

This is what I learned the hard way—a real big rude awakening for me. I used to love to share advice, talk about ideas and what I'm going to do and how I'm going to do it, looking for help from people competing with me. You're sharing your ideas, telling all these big aspirations and things you want to do in life, how you will get it done, and your plans. And you're sharing it with somebody genuinely that you're thinking is for you, but they compete with you. No matter how much help you're looking for from this person or how much support you're looking for from this person, they'll never give it to you because they feel like you're going to be bigger than them.

Everybody can't go. Just because people look good or have a nice financial setup doesn't mean they are supposed to go with you. That's what I mean by everybody can't go. Where God is taking you, they may not be room for people you are trying to bring.

Not just in a bad sense. Sometimes people can't go; that's right around you because where your harvest is, how you set up, and what's meant for you, it is not for them.

Learn how to love yourself before you can even figure out how to love anything else. Learn how to love yourself. Understand self-accountability. Do you know why? Because sometimes you can't go. What God has planned for somebody else, where they are in their lives, and the steps they are getting ready to take are not designed for you, and sometimes you can't go. Sometimes I can't go.

The longer you procrastinate and deal with something that isn't for you, the longer you postpone what is. That's the longer you take to get to what is for you. I used to go by an old saying that led me to believe, 'If it ain't making me no money, it ain't making me happy; time to stop making time for it.'

People are waiting to see if you will make it first before they support you. Everybody can't go. So, you have to realize that when a person is in and out of the car. When they are holding on to see it's going good, it looks like you are about to break through. It looks as if your business is about to prosper, and your career is about to take off.

You are giving up a little bit. You aren't working hard as you used to. People aren't all over you like that. I'm on to the next one; I'm out of the car. People are waiting to see if you will make it before they support you some time. They can't go.

Sometimes you have to fall back and let them run behind and lean on the ones they think highly of—the ones where the grass looks so green on the other side. Sometimes you got to let them do that, and God will send you a stranger to help you. I'm talking about sending you a stranger, have you networking with strangers, working outside of friends and family; he'll send you a stranger and takes you to the next level when people thought they were holding you back, from them not giving you, their help. It'll happen.

Sometimes, you have to leave the people you love and find those who love you. Find the people that appreciate what you do. Find the people that are grateful for what you bring to their life or bring to the table. Everyone's not appreciative and grateful. Some people are just courteous. It's a difference between the two.

Everybody can't go.

Now, let's go back to the stranger thing because it can be the other way around. People sometimes like to stay on top of you. They like to stay financially, socially ahead of you, whatever it is. It could be fashionably ahead of you. It's just people who like to keep you where you are based on your friendship or relationship; it could be whatever. And sometimes, these people will pass a great opportunity to a stranger just because they know your work ethic; they know your ambition is something that gets you to the next level. And it's people who are withholding an opportunity from you. You know, the people that can't go.

People will do that because they don't want to see you surpass where they are. So, they'll give that play to a stranger, something that was right by you.

But then it's not always about that. That's not playing the victim all the time, even with myself. At times, I was still on drugs, smoking, and drinking, not where I was supposed to be financially. There was an opportunity that passed me by because I wasn't ready, and I couldn't go.

The fellas were taking a couples trip, and they've been ready to enjoy themselves as married couples, and sometimes where you are at and what you still doing and the way you're living your life, you can't go. It's been times that I couldn't go. I couldn't go financially; I wouldn't be ready, I couldn't go mentally, I wouldn't be ready. I couldn't go socially; I wouldn't be ready. Sometimes you can't go.

Sometimes where God is taking you, ain't no room for nobody but you. Sometimes where God taking them, ain't no room for nobody but them. And then sometimes, where God takes us, ain't no room for nobody but us. And people have to understand that sometimes they are losing this opportunity or losing this great shot, and moving along in life is worth losing because of everybody that I want to take with me because it just might not be their time to go. Or, am I strong enough with enough faith and real enough to recognize when it's somebody else's time to go, understand that I can't go? Or am I willing to crash the ship or wreck the train just because I cannot go and it's somebody else's chance to be great? Everybody can't go.

You must know when it is and when it isn't your time to go. And be strong enough to know that your time is coming. We must stop losing relationships, or friendships, whatever it is in life and business, from going to bat for people you know wrong. You know everything about what they are saying or what they are doing is not right. But you are willing to go to bat for it and lose your credibility and respect from people just based on being cool or family.

See, when people ask you to risk something that means something to you; risk your career or opportunity, they can't go. You can't take them with you. People will ask you to sacrifice your self-respect; sacrifice your dignity, you know, give up everything that you stand for to get them where they need to go. They can't go.

Listen, they can't go and check this out right here. The money can be good. We are eating nice food. We are taking nice trips, but I got to stroke your ego, and you got to humiliate me every chance. I can't go. I don't go. If I got to lose respect, if I got to let you talk to me how you want to, kick me in my ass every time you get ready, I can't go.

You have to watch who you build with. Sometimes people will use you for the foundation. They'll use you to lay the foundation but finish the structure with somebody else. Somebody that didn't pick up a brick. Somebody that didn't pick up a hammer. It didn't help, but they'll finish the structure with them, so you have to watch who you build with. See, moving on and everybody can't go. That are two different things. Moving on is one thing. Moving on and knowing who you can't take with you or what you can't take with you is another thing.

Know when to go for it. Know when to take a chance. Know when to spend your last. Sometimes when you're doing that, you get to know when to leave somebody. Sometimes leaving it all on the field to get where you need to go, you may have to leave somebody. Everybody can't go.

I've been in situations where I've taken people's time for granted; where I've been very inconsistent, I might have been inconsistent with people's feelings and emotions. Time has passed, I've matured, and I'm different. I am reliable now. I am a much better person. I want to fix the mistakes, but God has moved them past that time. He moved their life forward in that business deal. I didn't get to go. Now it's up to me to be responsible and be real enough to accept that I wasn't ready; no blaming, no point feelings, looking myself in the mirror and knowing that I wasn't ready to go at that particular time.

I remember being unable to go as a kid because of my behavior. I was a class clown, talked too much, was always into something, and made jokes. Now it's time to go on the field trip, and you can't go based on your behavior.

This transitions as you get older. Now you get drunk and argue and fight at the party. You start talking about people, you can't control yourself, and this behavior removes you from the invitation list. You aren't invited to functions because of your behavior. Still 15, 20 years later. At some point, it can be your friends, family, loved ones, spouse, kids, or yourself. If you can't be entrusted or trusted in every environment that you need to have them around, they can't go.

Know your personality. Know your traits. Know what you like. If you like to smoke cigarettes and there are no cigarettes involved. You're either not going to go or not going to smoke. Know when you are supposed to go and know when you can't. I had to tell myself, 'Hey, listen.

If your religion is this, and they will be talking about something over here at this particular place that's going to go against what you believe in, don't go.' Don't be controversial; start a big ruckus and start a big argument in a place you didn't belong. Decide for yourself sometime when you can't go.

And last but not least, closing out, on everybody can't go... Make sure you don't leave the right people. Make sure that sometimes the right people go with you when you move on. Don't leave your blessing. Don't take somebody with you that ain't supposed to go, and be smart and unselfish enough to know you can't go by yourself. Make sure you take the right people with you. Make sure you do take the people that deserve to go with you. Make sure you do to people that earn your loyalty your trust whatever it was, stay down however you judge them. Make sure you take the right people that were supposed to go. This doesn't mean that nobody is supposed to go. "Everybody can't go" means when you can't go and when you have to move on away from people or just things. It's not always a people. Sometimes, it's your attitude that can't go; your selfishness can't go; you have too much pride that can't go; you have to leave that behind sometimes. Everybody can't go.

CHAPTER 7

INSTANT GRATIFICATION

It's people that are trading their happiness. You know they'll give up their financial security. A good income that's going to take care of their family. All for 10 minutes of fame. We live in a time when popularity and being socially accepted are glorified for worldly things. That's way bigger than hard work. Having a great work ethic that's a thing of the past. People want instant gratification.

We're not in a time when kids want to be lawyers, doctors, accountants, or dentists. The social media era is all instant gratification. Now it's all about being models and managers, talent, hosts, entertainers, designers, and promoters. People want to go to the top and get 15 minutes of fame overnight.

People don't have the patience to be great. They want to be bigger, better, and equal to their peers, friends, enemies, and coworkers; they want to do that now. You know, the time of working 24/7, 24/8, 365, 7 days a week, grind, grind, grind. No. Instant gratification.

I got bad news. Everybody ain't made to be an entrepreneur. I didn't say you couldn't be a winner. I didn't say you didn't have the opportunity to be great. I just said everybody wasn't made to be an entrepreneur. People leave their jobs after years of training and climbing the ladder in their profession. Hours and days of school, student loans, and hard work. People will leave all that to test out to be an entrepreneur. I didn't say an investor; I said an entrepreneur. And sadly, they do it for instant gratification.

Right now, people are risking it all just for that feeling of being a boss, to say they own something: logos, T-shirts, websites, and new social media pages. Many people chase that feeling, not to make generational wealth for their family, not something they are passionate about. For instant gratification, that comes with people viewing them as a boss. That's the time we're living in. You have to stop selling perception. People will believe in something they want to think is a reality, but it's not. I'm not telling you not to step out on faith. I'm not saying you got to work for somebody forever. That's not what I'm saying. I'm not saying don't leave it all on the field. I'm saying people are designed to be entrepreneurs based on the popularity that comes with it.

Going to work 12 hours a day to be in the crowd and spending money to look like CEOs, hang around athletes, and be like entrepreneurs, but you're not making any money off the game you're trying to play. People are spending their last on pictures. People are spending their last on the moment. Traveling out of town spending all types of money, not even worry about the enjoyment or the relaxation, just for the pictures.

I'm not telling you don't make memories. I'm telling you, do not live a life where you are giving up everything you got for a lane that might not be for you.

Being an entrepreneur takes a special kind of mind frame. When it comes to dedication when comes a work ethic a discipline. You have to understand to be self-employed because you got to know it comes with a lot of disappointment. People want to be self-employed and want to be entrepreneurs, but they hate bad news. Everybody is trying to get rich quickly based on the time and looking on social media. But the thing about it, you didn't work for the money, so you don't know what to do with it.

You have the drive, passion, talent, and support to jump out. I'm not killing your dreams. People have great things going on in life, but watching social media entrepreneurs and athletes makes them want someone else's life; they are willing to give up everything they have, and you can't do this for likes, followers, praise, and pats on the backs, instant gratification.

I was always caught up with instant gratification because I was extremely impatient. Over time and as you mature, you get a little bit more patience, and your patience improves. But as a young entertainer, very, extremely impatient.

See, instant gratification is not always material. It's not always a social feeling that you're looking for. It doesn't have to be related to looking good. It doesn't have to be about letting people shine. I wanted instant gratification from a woman. I've done this, I've done that. Why haven't you done this? Instant gratification.

I see it in many young artists and a lot of entertainers. "Hey, I'mma go to studio. I'mma do a song, do a video, put it out. I'm ready to go to the top. I'm ready to do shows and get the money." Instant gratification.

Hey man, I just dropped my first YouTube. My first single is out. I'm ready to start wearing Gucci belts, flying, first-class, and doing shows. Instant gratification.

The hard work is staying up three nights, leaving on February first and coming back on June 15th. I had seven friends, and I can only take one of them; you see, they're not considering that part of it, just the instant gratification.

Same thing with women. Women will go on three dates and be ready to get married. I've been out with him for two months. I'm ready to tie the knot because of the ring, the show, and the instant gratification that comes with the announcement, not the love, the fame, and the glory that comes with it. That's instant gratification.

I'm not saying that's the case for everybody. I'm not even saying you don't deserve to have success when you want it or when you desire it. We're talking about leaving great situations, turning away from promising futures to say you're a boss. It doesn't interest you, but it seems like it draws much attention and praise, so you want it.

I'm not raining on your parade. I'm not because I didn't say don't invest. I didn't say don't play your part, nor did I say don't take chances. I said have a realistic conversation with yourself before you decide to give up on the dreams you already worked your ass off for, just for instant gratification.

Sometimes the stuff you are going to do for people you love to help or look out for them, the feeling of what you want them to do will be wishful thinking. We are looking for instant gratification from these people and trying to get it out of them with a gift. Or the speech you didn't give them, a new car, a purse. A nice little quickie in the morning with your partner doesn't change who they were yesterday. Stop looking for instant gratification from people you can't even provide yourself.

People don't change overnight. Sometimes you have to have patience, but people think they can materially or financially stop someone from being who they were— looking for instant gratification, trying to buy your way out of it isn't going to work.

That's even in business. You got to be realistic and make it make sense. You got your car over here at the shop; it's been over there three-four months. They've been asking you to bring this money, material, and parts for months. You aren't answering the phone; you aren't picking up, and you aren't calling back. Finally, you get the money together, go over there and pay the mechanic, pay the workers to get it done, and you are ready for it to be done Friday. You want instant gratification now that you have paid your money. But what about the other four months when you had everything behind and all the people that just skipped you.

People want what they want when they want it and how they want it, so they can show it when they want to, but you got to work for it, and everything isn't about, you know the glory that's going to come right after you do it. Sometimes you have to work in January to see the results in November. Sometimes you have to stay up 24 hours, and you might not see that result until six months. Nothing happens overnight.

The fame and glory that your friends and peers get from doing what they do and how people love and respect and admire them for what they do. That doesn't mean you will get that same thing when you do that, and vice versa. People are ready to trade in their life for a life that they think is better than theirs. And people will love to be not stressed out. People will love to be, you know, comfortable and able to share their family and eat at the table. Sometimes what you have is much more gratifying than what you think the next person has. But you're looking at the way they're getting viewed, you're looking at the way they are getting liked, you're looking at the way they are getting supported, and you're ready to trade in all your hard work and what you've done for that, when in reality that person may envy the lifestyle that you've got.

The opposite of IG that I call instant gratification is trusting the process, being patient for the glory and fame that's coming to you anyway if it's meant for you. See, I slowed down on IG and stopped rushing to get accolades from people, stopped rushing the praise, when I realized I hadn't missed anything that God had for me; I hadn't missed anything that God wanted me to have. Sometimes, I wanted things early in my life, but I wasn't mature enough for them. Money, business, relationships, bills I wanted all these things, but I wasn't ready for them. Now, the gratification I get comes from the hard work, the understanding, and the lessons I got from going through it.

If you want to be an entrepreneur, do it. If you want to be self-employed, go for it. Do it for love, though. Do it for the change you will bring to people's life. Do it because you want to inspire. Don't do it because you want to shine this weekend. Don't do it because your friend did it or your family member is asking you to do it. IG is a gift and a curse. It may feel good at the moment. But will it last forever? Instant gratification.

We are going to close on a positive note. Let me tell you how to make IG work for you. Tell yourself you love yourself some time, instant gratification. Open up a door for a lady at the store, instant gratification. Pay your bills on time with instant gratification and a nice home-cooked meal with your feet on your table. Pray to God, ask him for what you want, and believe it's going to happen, instant gratification.

The bottom line, life is what you make it. People pick what they want to understand and what they don't. Nobody's telling you not to have a great time. Put your dreams aside to go work for other people. I'm saying be realistic. I love what you do. Be willing to work hard for it. And understanding that success and shine will not happen overnight. And sometimes, you have to be appreciative and grateful for the hard work that you put in. Be appreciative of yourself and not give up on that for instant gratification.

CHAPTER 8

ASSETS & LIABILITIES

When creating your business portfolio, investments, real estate, cars, and jewelry, all those are called assets and liabilities. But see when you're doing your life portfolio, your friends, your family, your people, habits, even decisions, see them also assets and liabilities.

Let's start right here. Including myself now. Men can be hustlers, great providers, and leaders, but in some areas of our life, we are just dumb as a bag of rocks. Some could have all the money in the world but can't book a flight, make an appointment or keep track of their health. But see this woman, she going to get your car note straight. When you're paying too much on your insurance, she will get on the phone with the people and argue all day with the light people and the cable.

Like this woman, when your baby mama didn't want to comb your little girl's hair and still sent her over there; this woman, she is going to get that done for you. That job you are trying to get, she is going to do that resume for you. This woman is a great asset to you, whether you want to believe that or not. In contrast, this other woman is great in the bed. You look good together when you're going out, and she the perfect eye candy. But she doesn't have any hustle. She loves to eat well and look fabulous. It's costing you half your profit and all your time. That's a liability. This is not a shot at pretty and fine women, sexy women, because a woman that's an asset to you can also be pretty and fine.

The same thing goes for these women. Baby, you got three kids. Three different fathers. One in jail. One that moved on and one we don't know where he at. But this new has accepted your flaws. He's providing for you and your kids, spent time with you, took all of you places as a family, and even prayed with you holding your hand. Please recognize this as an asset in your life. Please.

Now see on the flip side of that. Then there's the man with three kids and three different baby mamas, though. In between jobs, in between hustles. See, he got you where you can't work. You're losing weight, your family, your friends, everybody upset, everybody mad, you can't focus, you can't concentrate on your job, at your house, you depressed. This is a liability to you and your happiness.

See, we all need this asset right here. The one that helps us make better decisions. See, that's an asset. Because you never know if you are an asset or a liability in somebody else life. It's not always about money— wins, losses, or what you brought to the table. See, for me, good karma. I believe in the power of prayer. So having good people praying for me and wanting to see me win. That's an asset for me. Just like drugs and bad habits and drinking addiction, sex addiction is a liability if it's stopping you from moving forward in life.

Sometimes you can be on a selfish mission. It is not on purpose, maybe not even intentional. You may just be looking out for yourself the best way at the time. I've been there. I swear I've been there. Trying to bounce back from losses and the bad situation you were in. But at the time, you're selfish; you're a liability.

It's people who are going to show up on a rainy day. It's people who are going to still help you even though you let them down. Who is going to give you their last and not tell nobody? They went to war with you, but they told you when they were wrong. That's an asset to your life. See, a lot of people think about the plugs and hookups and certain things like that. They think that's an asset. Yeah, it can be, but that is temporary or for the moment.

I'm talking about something happening to you today, and this person here is taking your kids, treating them as their kids, and raising them when you're gone. That's an asset. It's bigger than money. Sometimes you don't have the skill or the training or the degree. But you're a fast learner; you're on time, so you got the bigger position. Your hard work, drive, motivation, and work ethic were an asset to you. In the same breath, I'm talking about in the same sentence; the one with the skill, the training, and the degree, you're lazy though, inconsistent, and not inspired. Even though you're smart, you can't get the job done. You're a liability. Assets and liabilities.

If you have the energy, the vibe, the spirit, the skill, whatever it is. To uplift people, you make people around you better; if you can inspire and motivate your surroundings and your environments, that's an asset, making people go harder or want better for themselves. If you believe in yourself enough to share your game or be open with people about life without being scared of what the opinions will be, that's an asset.

Sometimes, people keep reminding you of who you used to be—holding you hostage to your past. That's what I call it. They will tell you everything they do for you, everything they help you with. They are going to find ways to mention your failures. That's a real-life liability right there. One of the main and most important assets for me was my mind. That's what we are talking about assets and liability. One of my main and what should be one of your main assets is your mind and how you control it. See, having a gun or a pistol is not the only way to protect yourself. It's your instincts. Some parts of the game got to be finesse. Too much force and overpowering, that's a liability on whatever you are trying to get done. And at the same time, let's keep it 100. And at the same time, your mind can be a liability too, when you're overthinking everything. Just because you can't trust one person doesn't mean everybody is out to get you. Sometimes it's your mindset that is your biggest liability. You're stopping yourself from getting yourself where you are trying to go. Your thought process, your negative outlook on everything. Your mind not being an asset to you.

See, you may have all the desire and all the intentions to get something done that you need to do, and you may eventually do it. But you are deciding to hire or ask for help to get it done in a timely fashion or to get it done the right way; that's an asset. Sitting there procrastinating, instead of telling yourself you are going to do it, that's a liability to whatever purpose you have for whatever you were trying to do. Yeah, that's that decision-making asset we are going to talk about. But check this out.

As soon as you are old enough to understand what's going on out here, or as soon as you become a parent, as soon as you start a job, or a career, one of your first assets should be insurance. Yeah, number one is life insurance. Insurance on everything that you work for that you want to protect that's fine. But a major asset should be life insurance. See, because what you have and what you want people to believe you or what you don't have and what people believe you do or don't. Whatever that is. That's wishful thinking. But to secure that asset, you get your friends and family a full break from heartache when you die. Just because you know you don't want to be a liability when it's all over.

Get some insurance. That's a major asset. And we are not just talking about car insurance, rental insurance. Put some insurance on your decisions. You know, that means you are willing to cover, you know what I'm saying; that means you are willing to fix anything you decide to do at all cost. That's when your decisions become an asset to you. Assets and liabilities.

When you decide that you are too tired of being used, when you decide to say no to somebody, say that. When you decide to do something and are willing to stand on it and for whatever you believe in and can deal with the consequences, your decisions start becoming an asset to you. Now, when you let people make you do things you don't want to do, or better yet, you just got a whole lot of shit that you want to do; you're real indecisive... in your marriage, your career, you personally; you don't know what you want to do. I've been there. I know how I feel. So, you decide to do whatever you see everybody else doing. That's when your decisions begin to become liabilities for you.

After I figured out how to start becoming a winner and God started blessing me with some success in my profession, people will start telling you they love you. It's going to be a lot of praise. A lot of fame and glory. They start saying, 'Lil Keke, he a legend.' And that's a great feeling. But over the years, I found out that one of my biggest assets was my accepting the other part. Yeah, the hate, the ridicule, the negative comments, the criticism, the backstabbing. See, I'm not saying I mastered it or was always ready for it, but once I understood that it wasn't one without the other, it became one of my greatest assets.

Success got a nasty side to it. If your skin is thin, your ego bruises easily; if you don't like no or disappointment; you're scared of failure; then your character is a liability in the world of being an entertainer or entrepreneur or even, for the most part, self-employed. Figure out what's your assets and your liabilities.

I've seen situations where a lot of times people start businesses, they finally get the opportunity to start a business, you finally get yourself rolling, and the first thing you want to do is hire your partner; you know, your homegirl, your auntie, your uncle. Yeah, that's cool. But he smokes all day, owes two bonds, and has already been to prison before. He's a liability.

This person may go to war with anybody for you at any time. His loyalty is an asset to your life but hiring him to work at your business that's a liability. Yeah, you can have both at the same time. They can go hand in hand, assets, and liabilities. See your homegirl; you trust her to keep your kids. She'll drive state to state, city to city with you. Fight everybody in the club with you. Ride with you when you're wrong and tell you when you're wrong simultaneously. Her love is an asset to you, but she is lazy. She loves to get high. And on occasion, she might steal. She is going to be a liability to your business. You must understand your assets and liabilities when it comes to decision-making.

One of my liabilities, especially in my career, was worrying about the wrong thing and waiting on certain things. That was a liability for me because it stopped me from seeing the bigger picture or missing out on what was meant for me anyway.

See, sometimes, when you are a self-employed entrepreneur, especially in entertainment, you look for people you want to support you, people you want to have favor and recognition from. People you think are important and what knowing them is going to bring to your presence. And then, when it doesn't go your way, it becomes a liability to your focus. That was when I realized that every person I felt should have supported me or people I was expecting mutual pay from because I thought they were so big and so impressive, it was 5 or 6 people. Not as shiny as them, but they were supporting my brand wholeheartedly without me even asking them, and that's when I realized that these people were the real assets to my career.

Assets and liability. Things that will bring you favor, love, loyalty, compassion, and things that will stop you from getting where you're going. Stop you from rising. Stop you from conquering your battles or getting to whatever you're trying to get to. Figure out your assets and liabilities.

CHAPTER 9

BOTH SIDES OF THE LINE

Some people like to play both sides of the line. Then again, you could be a person that respects and understands both sides of a line. See, that's two different things. Okay, we will start right here; you have to watch people who like to hang with people they constantly talk bad about. No, for real. That's why it's really good to shut down hating conversations before they even start. Don't even play both sides of that line. And you don't always have to react to everything that you notice. Sometimes keep it moving.

Play crazy sometimes to the people that already think you're crazy. You know, both sides of that line. You don't have to tell everything you have going on in your life. When you stop doing that, most of the things that you work for and pray for will start coming quicker. Draw a line in the sand with that early. If you are praying to remove people from certain situations in your life, crying out for help from God, then when he rescues you from it, take it away, take that out of your life, and you go right back to it. That's both sides of the line. One side of the line is the intentions you may have to get some done, and the other is what you want to do—both sides of the line.

Stop worrying about who is coming back and focus on who stayed. I remember when I started putting in my prayers, 'God, please let me be ready for all these things that I'm praying for.' Because those prayers only work if you believe in them, faith.

If I'm fixing to work hard and pray even harder for something, it's playing both sides of the line if I don't believe it can happen.

Let me put this on your mind. Some people are going to love you no matter what you do. And then some people aren't going to never love you no matter what you do. Figure out how to love yourself. Because people will put you dead last in their lives, I'm talking about the bottom of the barrel. But when they need something, you are the first one they call. Keep that same energy. That's both sides of the line.

Here's how you play both sides of the line from a positive standpoint. This is how you be on the positive side of the line. By knowing it's okay to clap, it's okay to clap for your friends if their dream takes off before yours. Yeah, it's okay to support their success, knowing it doesn't get in your way. That's playing both sides of a good line and supporting people knowing that you will eventually get where you are supposed to get anyway.

Not all the time, but a lot of times, with three best friends, it's a good chance somebody will end up playing both sides. When two of your partners, two of your homegirls, and two of your associates become enemies, choose what's right. Let the truth guide your decision. See, if you feel sorry for one, you're comforting them through it, but the other one is wrong, but they do more for you; so, you agree with them to not lose them; you're playing both sides. You don't always have to pick a side. Just pick what's right.

Shannon Sharp says, "two things can be right." Stop playing both sides of the line, with your hustle, with your money; either you want it, or you don't. People do the bare minimum and are expecting great results.

You know, here goes my golden rule for me. 'He who makes the gold makes the rules.' I'm not crossing that line right there. It would help if you stopped acting like you were happy for your people's success. But you are telling everybody they think they are better than everybody else.

See, people do you wrong, and then they'll call you or like your post or something, start some small talk to see if you know what happened or if you are really mad—checking pulses, checking temperatures, playing both sides of the line.

See, if you have such a genuine heart for helping, helping people, and helping your coworkers, why are you telling everything you do? If you are going to have sex with your supervisor's husband, don't go to lunch with her anymore. That's both sides of the line.

Me, I've been in the middle before between friends. Instead of me being the one that just told them the truth from the beginning, I got one I'm trying to keep happy, so I'm telling them what they want to hear. I got the other one. I'm trying to keep them happy, so I'm telling them what they want to hear. They both end up mad at me for not being honest from the gate about how I felt about the situation. I chose to play both sides. It was a mistake.

I realize that sometimes you can't have the same relationship with two different people. The way they see each other and the way they see you may be different. The only thing that you can choose is what's right on your behalf. That's when you pick the right side of your line.

Check this out right here. You can't be riding with your partner all day, you know, your man's, this your dog, this your brother. But you're pillow talking with your girl and sharing information that you know about his life, but your girl is going to tell his. Then you get back in the car with him and sympathize with what he is going through—playing both sides of the line, along with a few other things you're doing.

Sometimes when your friends know too much about your business, it leads them to sympathize and have compassion for your situation in times they really shouldn't. It makes them play both sides. See, it's a sad thing. But sometimes, you got to pick a side and stay there. We all play both sides when it comes to love or even relationships. See, you want to be free, single, social, independent, all this in the public eye. But then you want to be cared for, loved, and hold hands behind closed doors. See, that's playing both sides.

Be honest and upfront with people; tell them your intentions and give them the chance to make a decision. Now for anybody, if you continue to do something that you don't like or don't make you happy, don't blame the other person for your decision. That isn't their fault. You're playing both sides, or with your decision, that's what you are doing.

I know me, and I'm not the only one. You play both sides with your kids in so y kinds of ways. See, I don't know if it's good or bad, but for instance, say a teacher call and says something bad and a little harsh about your kid. Now, I know my child; for the most part, I know what they are capable of; you know that's still my baby.

So, of course, I'm going to get on my kid, but yeah, I need to have another chat with that teacher too. That's me; I got to play both sides of that. If you are going to be cool, nice, friendly, and cordial at the job, at church, and in any of the places, don't shit on your coworkers when you see them in public because you're with your big-time friends, then go back to work, and you know you want to be cool again. That's playing both sides.

Now see this one for me right here. If you have certain people, you hang with or are with, that's not going to allow you to speak to me or talk to me because you're with them; it isn't any need of you speaking to me when you're by yourself. That's both sides of the line. Here's how you can play both sides of the line easily and positively. Be neutral sometimes, be even kilt. Keep your opinions and advice to yourself, especially when you're not asked. Let people work out their problems. Sometimes you have to listen and be quiet and move past it. You heard what they both had to say, and then you let them work it out. You play both sides of that line.

Know when to turn it on and off. You can't be the same person in every situation. I'm not telling you to compromise your character or your personality. I'm saying the same ruthless dictator you might have to be at your job; you may not have to use the same tactics at home. Confusing people you don't know or care anything about with the ones you love at your house is playing both sides of the line. A very thin line at that. Know when to turn it on and off. Every situation and every scenario in your life doesn't require you to be the same person.

Some things can be good for your soul; others can be good for your happiness so that it can be good for your career. That's men, women, attorneys, and people in general. But I had to stop playing both sides of that. And I started respecting and figuring out which lines not to cross.

But okay, here goes a good line to cross through right here. No matter how much you look up to or respect and admire a person, I know when to stand up for myself and mine. And for my family or my spouse or whatever it is. That's when you play both sides of the line. No matter how much respect I got for you and look up to you, I'll never let you play me. I respect you, but I will stand up for mine when it's time. That's playing both sides of the line.

Here is a killer for you when you want your friends and your family to do good but not better than you. You are playing both sides. When you don't want a person in your life, you do enough just so nobody else won't have them—playing both sides of the line. One of my biggest faults is having great talks, great intentions for something, and engaging in it but knowing I don't have the time for it, or I can be all in it to get it done. But I'm still holding on to the thought of it and playing both sides.

It's not always about playing both sides of the line. Sometimes it's about just understanding and respecting the side of a line you may have to pick. When you're picking or choosing a side of a line, don't let it dictate your character or make you lose respect for yourself or, the main thing, disrespect other people. If you figure out what's right, not who, but what's right, which sometimes may be you minding your own business, that's going to allow you to play both sides of any line.

Just figure out what's your bottom line. That way, you'll know which side you have to play and which you don't.

Both sides of the line.

CHAPTER 10

KEEP YOUR GRASS CUT & SWEEP YOUR OWN PORCH

Keep your grass cut and sweep your own porch first. See, it isn't just about the snakes when you're doing your yard. What about the leeches, freeloaders, deadbeats, complainers, people who want entitlement, bad energy, sometimes all that? See your energy in your space and your comfort zone; that's your yard. Keep your grass cut so you can see just what's in there. At the same time, sweep your porch first. Take care of your business. Get your yard straight. Get your situation straight before you can start giving people advice about theirs. That's cleaning your closet.

Sometimes decisions you make, or the choices you will have to make, will be based on what you need to do for your character. Do you get what I'm saying? Don't compromise who you are just because of what somebody else will do. See me; I get my blessings based on what I do. I will not lose what God got for me or do evil for evil because somebody is out of character. See, I clean my porch first. Because people love to judge you and assassinate your character for shit, they've done just like you, but there's a secret.

I had to stop holding grudges and start remembering facts. That's it. For instance, people this what they do; when they stop talking to you, they start talking about you. You got to watch them; keep your grass cut. I had to realize is it's not about the length of the friendship; it's about the strength of the friendship. You have people that do more for people and have a better respect for you in 5 years than somebody you probably knew for 20. See, once you start keeping your porch clean, staying on your game, and minding your business, you will learn to stop looking for yourself in other people, wanting them to do what you would. Accept people for who they are, not who you want them to be.

There will be all kinds of people in your yard. This, for instance, check this out:

"You call me 100 times when you're down, but when you were up, I ain't hear from you. But I got the same number. I got the same number."

I'm not here to talk about nobody. I'm no different than anybody else. We all need prayer. We all need some prayer. But you get tired of helping people that don't want to help themselves. How do I want to do more for you than you want to do for yourself? It can sometimes be a blessing in their face, but they just can't recognize it. Keep these kinds of people out of your yard. And for some people, it is people in competition with people that God sent to help them.

Your insecurities, attitude, and that hate in your heart; will hold you back from someone God has sent to help you. That's why you got to clean your porch. It isn't them all the time; sometimes it's you, it's your mindset.

I used to ask myself this, it's so crazy; 'why do people determine if they will forgive you based on how you are doing? Sometimes they'll forgive you because you're doing good. Everybody praises you; everybody likes you, so they forgive you too. Look, people do that. Cut your grass. Keep your yard cut. Watch them! Those are the sometimes.

I never understood why people worry about what's happening in a house where they don't stay. Sweep your porch. Why you got so much to say about these people's relationships or marriages, and you've been divorced two times. Sweep your own porch. Even I told myself when things weren't going my way, and I was doing bad in a relationship, or I didn't have a steady relationship at the time when I may be going through what I was going through. I had to tell myself that space in your bed sometime; that's a blessing. You could have something in there, something in your yard you don't even need.

Keep your yard cut. And at the same time, you are doing that sweep your porch. Judge yourself first before you judge somebody else. And don't forget, every once in a while, you will have to remind somebody to sweep their porch because they have selective memory, playing dumb and remembering what they want. Clean your porch. Clean your closet first.

Sometimes I see people right now who feel like they cut me off, not knowing I was praying for them to be out of my life the whole time. I have been working on my yard. I had years where I lost friends and money, but I know if God blocks it and remove it, then leave it alone.

I remember being mad at people because I didn't feel like they supported me the way I wanted them to, versus I didn't get back. When people didn't show up for parties and events I was having; I was in my feelings. But then I swept my porch and realized I had done many of the same things to people myself. Sometimes you have expectations for people when you think they're on a certain level. But you may have done the same thing to someone else who may not be on the same level as you, but it still counts.

It made me realize that sometimes people had to cut their grass and remove me from their yard.

That's when you have to realize stop calling people all the time when you need them. Call them to see if they need you for something. Keep your grass cut.

Watch people who tell you everything you do. Every single thing you do, they are telling it, but they never gossip about how you help them. They never tell that part.

Many people can't prosper because you're taking down too many good people while trying to get to the top. Yeah, because seeing for me, I can remember shit like no matter how much you look out for certain people, you can look out for them every day. They will still put people in front of you who did way less. And I'm not just talking about no financial either. But see, I had to learn this, cleaning out my closet; I don't have time to worry about somebody else's skeletons if I'm cleaning my closet.

Sometimes, your yard can be filled with negative energy, disruptions, and hate, and you can't get where you need to go. This happens because you must stop telling people more than they need to know. And stop showing them more than what they need to see. Keep your yard cut.

When your grass is too high, you need to cut it so you can see the blessings under there. Once again, it's not always about the snakes, the takers, or your grass from a negative standpoint. You got to water it. You got to fertilize it. Good people surround your yard so your flowers can grow. That's why you surround your yard with good people. Sweep your porch. Take care of your business so your business can take care of you. That's rule number one.

God removed certain people from your life, from your yard, because he heard a conversation you didn't. Don't question that. People can have way more than you have. I'm talking about ten times and still be jealous of you. Your mystique, your aura, the way people envy you, the way people love you, the way people treat you. They can have way more than you and still be jealous of you.

I saved a lot of reputations. I saved a lot of reputation because I didn't tell my side of the story. You know, thank me later. People are always sorry when you find out what they say. Soon as you find out, I'm sorry, but you weren't sorry when I didn't know.

Take your time and do a self-check. Check your ego. Check your attitude. Take some of your blame. I like to recognize my faults and sweep my porch. People respect you differently when you can admit your wrongs. When you can stand in front of your failures and stand in front of your fault, you know, accept yours.

You are sweeping up your porch. You don't need anybody to do that for you. Why has somebody got to come in your yard and sweep your porch?

You also want to watch your surroundings. Move things out of your space that will hurt you, be against you, or not in your favor. Have your shit together so you can keep your yard straight, and you won't have to watch somebody else's. See, it's people who prey on the weak. It's people who benefit from your lack of knowledge. And it's just straight-up people who want your spot. They want your spot; they are in your yard. But if you just cut it and remove them and make room, you will get that spouse who will help you grow. Now you will get that financial blessing that's on the way to make you win yard of the month!

The moral of the story is to protect your energy. Keep your space clear and recognize what you are supposed to do and how long you are supposed to be there and what is not supposed to be in your life so that you can make room for the things that are supposed to be there. The things that are going to help you grow. At the same time, have your affairs in order before you can judge somebody else's.

Keep your grass cut and sweep your porch.

CHAPTER 11

TRADING PLACES

You have to figure out what's a fair trade for you before giving up something and being in a place you never wanted. This chapter is about different trades that you can make in your life. But at the same time, it's about being in the wrong place at the wrong time and understanding that's how you catch an out-of-place case.

Why do people from great families with a solid support system so desperate to trade that in to see what the other side feels like? Your parents, people, and loved ones have been through hell and back, having made all kinds of sacrifices to get you the help and resources you need to make the road a little lighter for you... People trade that in for the struggle, thinking I don't want any help. I don't need it. I'm doing it all by myself. Man, that's cool, but you ain't built like that. You weren't raised under those kinds of circumstances. That mindset doesn't even fit the lifestyle that you came up under. You come from a situation where you are now trying to get credit, recognition, and cool points from people who have been through things that you have never been through.

Ready to catch an out-of-place case. Sometimes you have to stay in your jurisdiction. Take advantage of the opportunity that has been given to you. That means even if it's helping, pulling up, saving people that you know, that's cool. But don't trade in your blessing to experience some shit that you think will improve your story.

Out of place case is people who think the only way to come up is to have a sad story to go with it. Everybody hated on me. The teacher said I wasn't going to make it. Man, ain't no whole lot of teachers said that. That's been said probably two out of 10 times you've heard it. See, those out-of-place cases will have you trading places every day. That's beyond super uneven, ain't bringing no balance to your life.

For instance, here we go... Stop trading respect for money. I don't care what kind of money we are getting or what kind of revenue you are turning me on to; if I got to let you belittle me, disrespect me, you know what I'm saying, just because you pay good, I can't make that trade.

People love the term "fake it till you make it," but the term respect is non-negotiable in every deal. Soon as it starts with disrespect, deal off. Because see, if you are a hustler, you will get a shot at some money anyway, but when people lose respect for you, you rarely get that back. If you're a hustler, you can get some money back, but you can't get that respect back. That will put you in the wrong place at the wrong time.

I've had conversations with people. You know, just life in general. One of the hardest things to do is trade in a place you're in for a place you want to be and then trade all that in for a place you need to be.

I was addicted to late nights, women, weed, drinking, smoking, riding clean all day, and the worst of all, loving it; until I lost everything. I had to trade it in for freedom, trade it for sanity, health and family. Best trade of my life, though. Because during one of the worst times of my life, I picked up one of my best attributes: don't wait for humble pie. Learn how to serve yourself before life does it.

I was always in the wrong place at the wrong time, steadily getting out of place cases; I had to trade that pride for a slice of humble pie. Yeah!

Let me turn you on to a mistake we all make that will put you in the wrong place when you trade happiness for love. Some people learn this late, and I don't know how long it will take you to figure it out. Ain't no love worth no ass-whooping. Ain't no love worth depression. Ain't no love worth suicide. How the hell are we in love and we mad and sad every day? I don't want any love that makes me feel good, but I have to hurt behind it.

No, let me say that right. You don't make me feel good, but I love you. I don't want to be with you, and we don't get a future, but I love you. I keep doing this shit out of love. That's a major out-of-place case.

Now here goes one that I'm telling you: the coldest one. I don't love or want to be with you, but I don't want anybody else to have you. You got to get out of that. If you mentally and physically know that's happening to you, you're saying; I'm willing to trade in my happiness for myself because I love you. Where they do that at? That ain't never been a fair trade.

One of the reasons for that is that people love to trade in their life or just their life situation for somebody else's based on how they see them living publicly. You don't have any idea what they got going on privately. You don't know what skeletons they got, what it took them to get there, who they are behind a closed door. You want their life. Look at their relationship; they are so in love, and they look so cute and perfect. But he got anger issues, and they got three domestic cases. Yeah, they are holding hands-on social media. Oh, they got such a big mansion; but they sleep in different rooms. They are not in love no more. They are not happy no more. They've traded that for perception.

Guess what we're saying? "They look happy. You know. I don't know if they are still in love, but they look happy." That's what we're saying. Stop trading in the happiness of your life for the love that you think somebody else is getting in theirs.

Be careful. Watch people who trade in their friends and family for new relationships—just for a come-up. See, that's trading loyalty for opportunities. Kings and queens give up their place on the board to be pawns. Just to be associated with people for popularity. Sharing some fame and light that they got isn't even yours.

People stop supporting their friends and their businesses so that they can help the competition flourish. Because the $10 is cheaper because they establishment looks so much nicer and is surrounded by so many more VIPs. People will give up their loyalty; they will be trading their loyalty, which will have you in the wrong place at the wrong time. Just eager and begging to be in rooms and places you don't even belong. Do you know what I'm saying? Them rooms that you're trying to get in and trading your loyalty for, the people in there, they're in there talking about how you did that out-of-place case.

There's nothing like trading something and ending up in the wrong place at the wrong time. You know, which will most likely lead to a nice out-of-place case—this one I recognized and started to see my maturity. When I started to cherish my peace and found a way to not trade my peace of mind for nothing, I knew I was growing. See, it could be from the smallest thing for me. From watching the football game, relaxing, cooking some good food, making my music, listening to some music, or you know, just whatever you do. You know; however, you enjoy your life and put your mind at ease.

Now, imagine this, just because you are having sex with somebody, it doesn't matter whether you're married; it could be your sneaky link, whatever you call it, or just your sex partner in general. Just because you are having sex, you have to trade in your peace of mind. You got to trade that all in for cursed-out text messages, 30-minute arguments on the phone, flat tires, busted windows, fights in the yard, and police coming. There's no way I'm trading in peace of mind for a piece of ass. I lost my sanity, all my time; I got to stay stressed out just because we were having sex? Nah, that isn't any fair trade.

Now I got an out-of-place case. How much of your peace are you willing to trade and give up for that temporary emotion? Like see, I like the way you make me feel. You make me feel good. You turn me on. But you like to argue, fight, and be toxic five days a week. I can't make that trade.

And I'm not trying to be funny. But the same thing for women. Stop trying to have kids with men you know you aren't going to be with. You have no future in hell with this person. I'm not saying break-ups; I'm not saying splits or separations. I'm talking about having raw sex with married men or men in a relationship because you like the idea of having a kid with him based on what he got. Now the baby got an out-of-place case before it even got here. And vice versa with men; trading their families, trading in their wives, good homes for women that they know if it were over with right now with your wife, you wouldn't be with this other woman tomorrow. A bad trade got you in the wrong place at the wrong time with an out of place case.

Sometimes we just got to make that decision for the kids before they even get here. Now check this out since we are talking about the kids and out of place cases. Fellas, tell me this... The baby is nine years old; it's his first game, his first little league game. It's 9 AM Saturday at the church park. Why did you get thousands of dollars worth of jewelry and two watches? Mama, why are you in Fendi boots with a Chanel bag? Now you're mad because all the parents are talking and whispering in the stands, but you got an out of place case. It's a time and a place for everything. That's why never trade your respect for attention. See, I'm not judging. Do as you please, but you have to be prepared for the backlash to go with it.

See, the internet is the biggest platform where we trade respectful attention. People with low self-esteem will give up self-respect just for people to like them. If they only knew there was a one-way street and a never-ending road, not an even trade. This is an actual trade; let me give you one. When you ask a person something, and they give you their honest opinion, honest opinion, and whether you like it or not, we still cool whether we don't agree. That's an even trade.

Sometimes you have to take your time to get to know people. Many people are so in a rush; they want to move so fast, just so desperate to be in a relationship because they envy their friend's situation, they want to be in love too. But everybody's situation is different. You may start with someone and jump right into it because you feel it. But this person can have baggage and history you are not even ready for.

People spend so much time in their life watching other people's love stories and trying to relate that to theirs, when in reality, when everything may unfold with the person you have, you could be in the wrong place at the wrong time. Sometimes you have to take your time instead of trying to trade in your situation for the situation that you are looking at that you think so much better.

Here's an out-of-place case for me; when I get mentally and socially, Nah, let me say this, it's when based on my career, I get culturally pressured and forced to do things I don't want to do. I'm pressured to be in places and around people I know don't want me there. But see, I got to participate for so many different reasons. Keep the chatter down; live and let go; let bygones be bygones. You're grown, you so much mature, but in reality, I got out of place case. I'm uncomfortable. I'm trading in my real feelings with fake ones. The older I got, I realized that wasn't a fair trade. But check this out; what if I traded places and I'm one of the ones in the room; what if the colleague, the coworker, the peer, or one of my partners walk in, and I don't feel the same way as the room do? But I'm in there, so I'm a part of the narrative. Wrong place, wrong time, out of place case. Do you know what I'm saying? What do you do about that?

The reason I brought that up is a very important part of this chapter that I want to talk about; watch the people who are part of the "hate team" the recruiting. Now that they're mad and moving on from a person, they're taking everybody with them. They are going to convince the rest of the team to follow suit. We're all mad at you! I've seen people fall right into that trap. They get an out-of-case place for joining someone else's business, which had nothing to do with you.

Now watch this. This is how they repay you. They go back to being friends with the person you turned everybody against. And see, for me, I know that they are coming back. Everyone was on the other side now, and I knew the person was coming back the whole time. Because see, what y'all thought he could do for you or what he was going to tell you, it couldn't help you. You traded your loyalty for an opportunity. They got you an out of place case.

Here's how we close out. We are all human, so being in the wrong place at the wrong time, is not when it's going to happen; it's when. Be careful when you're making trades. Look at the whole picture before you're so quick to trade places for different scenarios in your life. Ain't no attorney fees for out of place cases. You got to be your own judge and jury.

CHAPTER 12

THE CHOICE IS YOURS; LIVING OR EXISTING

The choice is yours. It doesn't matter if yesterday was a good or bad day; today is another opportunity for you to start living. People have just accepted failure. "I lost, I ain't trying no more; I give up; it what it is; I'mma work on this job and pay these bills and just live humbly," which is fine, ain't no problem with that at all. But before you got into this relationship, you had big dreams, major plans, and aspirations. But ever since you gave up on them, now you're just existing.

See, I've existed in a world where my love for my addictions and habits was way greater than me living righteously. I remember calling the light company, the cable company, whatever it was, to get an extension. You know so that I can drink and smoke. Give me some cool kicks, sweatpants, and a lot of white T-shirts. I didn't need to treat myself to no nice clothes; all I needed to do was get high. See, I've been there before you get to the point where all you want to do is enough. As long as your phone bill is paid, the car is straight, it got some gas, and you can get something to eat when you are high; well, you're good, existing; you're the Walking Dead.

But every day, God wakes you up the first thing you get is a choice. If you are alive and free, that's another opportunity to start living. Now, no matter how much money you're getting, what you're buying, how good life treats you, that's good, but that's not what we're talking about. I'm talking about speaking of living in, believing in yourself no matter how many times you fail, no matter how many times they tell you no, making peace with your past, and moving on and controlling your happiness; that's living.

No matter what we've been through as a person, the only respect that you owe people anyway is the respect that they are willing to show you. Don't let anybody steal your joy. It's somebody for everybody, keep doing you, somebody going to feel it. People worry themselves to death about things they have been through with people, and the people have moved on. You're creating unnecessary stress for yourself, and worrying doesn't do anything but intensify the problem. You're existing instead of living your life.

See, one thing about when you're the walking dead is so hard for you to see and figure out that people are doing the best for them. People love what's doing the best that's for them. Do you know what I'm saying? You're mad and in your feelings, but take advantage of your turn to do the best for you, what's best for you.

You're bitter, and they're living the sweet life. That choice is yours. It may take ten hard years to get that one that will change your life forever, but that one year can be the roadway to the next best ten you will have. Keep grinding; you don't know what year your year can be.

See, one thing I know for sure and that I was taught, a coward isn't going to ever start. Winners, we never quit, but the weak don't finish either. See, they never do. I remember all the doors closing on me. I'm talking about relationships with people; I'm on bad terms; all types of things are happening. But I didn't feel like I was getting what I deserved or earned. I was in my feelings and voicing it, voicing it as much as I could. One day my mentor told me, "Close your mouth and open my ears so that I can hear the next opportunity." Knocking. Close your mouth, and open your ears so you can hear the next opportunity knocking.

Just being truthful and honest, I did not start receiving everything in front of me until I started letting go of the things behind me. Now I'm living.

Make peace with your past, so you won't be the walking dead. That choice is yours. In 10 to 15 years, you want to have been and chose your life, not settled for it. People be giving up right before the miracle may be finna happen.

See, the one thing I know about just running through life and existing. You will find yourself building somebody else's dream while yours is forgotten.

Let's get this understood. This isn't for everybody, and that's okay. It isn't for everybody without no judgment. You can be content, satisfied, and happy in your own right. I'm not knocking that. I'm talking to the people who had so many great things ahead of them. Once, they had so many dreams they were working on and so many things they wanted to be in the future. Once it was derailed by one mistake or one person or one situation, you gave up on everything you prayed for. I'm talking to those people. Now you're the walking dead. But that choice is yours.

One of my favorite things is killing them with kindness and blindness. Yeah, I'm kind to you, but I'm also blind and not paying attention to that bullshit that you're doing. Yeah. Learn how to get up from tables that (no, don't get up) stop sitting at tables that soon as you get up, you're the topic. Yeah, it would be best if you found ways to live your life outside worrying about what everybody thinks about you. If you're affected by everybody's thought process and every word and everything to somebody, and it's going to hold you back, then you might want to remove yourself from the situation. Do what you need to do to get your mind right.

One of our biggest mistakes as people is saying yes to everything. Saying yes to things that you know you hate to do. And then you bring it back up when you're mad. Now you want to talk about the person and have many derogatory things to say. But you were the one who kept saying yes to something that you didn't want to do.

People give people so much freedom to treat them any kind of way. Then they turn around and get mad at that person because they are living their best life. You let them do that. You didn't make your own choice about what you want to do for yourself. You can also find people who are mad at you because of their situation; you're mad that it took you forever to get it done. They took it and made the best out of it. They are mad at you because you did that. You all come from the same type of situation that you have been complaining about and couldn't make any sacrifices for. They took that small amount, ran with it, and made something. And you're mad at that.

CHAPTER 12: THE CHOICE IS YOURS; LIVING OR EXISTING

This is how we are closing. Life is what you make it. If you want and desire better for yourself, you will put in your best effort. But when you feel entitled and like everybody owes you something, that world you lived in, that you existed in, it will be full of excuses. So, stop walking around dead behind some shit that died a long time ago. Your second chance in life is really up to you. You're either living or existing. The choice is yours.

People die at 25 but don't get buried until they are 75.

Because you are living or existing out here, we used to hear this all the time, but we don't understand it or fail to realize what it means. And that's, life is what you make it. The choice is yours. It's so many people that are miserable and left behind. I'm talking about still suffering from mistakes and missed opportunities that they had years ago. They had the slightest idea how to forgive themselves or give themself a second chance, waiting on somebody else to give them another chance at their own life. People will stay stuck in the dirt.

I'm talking about leaving them in the mud until someone saves them. But the cold part is they used all their energy and prayers to help other people get their second chances all the time but won't get their self-one.

Drowning in your sorrows is the walking dead. You're just existing, but life is what you make it. If you let it, two or three bad decisions can dictate the rest of your life. But you have to come to terms with that living in your guilt ain't going to change the past, so you can stop doing that.

Ain't no way to get to the next chapter of your life if you are still living in the last one. That's facts. We've heard this so many times. At least I have, and people think this is so cliche. Dust yourself off and get back up. If you fall seven times, get back up at eight. That's not a gesture. You have to train your mind into that being a way of life because life is what you make it. You're either living in your full potential, or you exist in your fear. You exist in doubt and are missing out on many things that you probably should have, making you the walking dead.

I've seen people lose half their life, never bounce back, behind a broken heart, behind a bad relationship. I'm talking about naturally getting hurt once and then missing out on everything else life offers. Now, they exist.

Sometimes you have to realize that it may break your heart, but it will open your eyes. Again, live and let go. I'm not telling you it's going to be easy. I'm not saying that. Let me tell you what somebody wise told me, plenty of wisdom. They said, "you'll never be good enough for the wrong person. Life goes on."

When you ask yourself, am I living or am I existing, rule number one should be to stop waiting for people to make you happy. Yeah, stop waiting for people to make you happy. Love is a great thing. We all want it, but not to the point where I depend on somebody else to make me happy. Not to the point where I depend on somebody to make me smile or have a good day. First of all, that's too much pressure on the other person.

I'm not saying couples and loved ones can't do things together that make each other smile or happy. I'm just saying; that I'm not going to let you control me to where if you don't do it, I'm not going to be happy. I can't eat unless we eat. I can't stop unless you're there helping me pick it out. If it's a joke that ain't funny to me, then it isn't funny to you. That's the walking dead, existing so miserably.

That was one of the best life lessons that I ever learned. Never put your happiness in somebody else's hands and let them decide when you will be happy. Start living. See, that's controlling your peace, protecting your energy, and being in complete charge of your happiness.

See, every time we talk about living, we talk about shopping, traveling, and having fun. I'm talking about living, having freedom, good favor, and respect from people. See, when your friends, family, and people you don't know start admiring your loyalty and how you keep it a hunnid. People start to want to help and bless you even more; that's living. But see, when you're the walking dead, you can't see it. You can't feel it. You're too bitter. You're holding grudges for people that's moved on. Start living; the choice is yours.

Check this out; people can be down the street from you; hell, next door and still won't support you. Nothing you do, but they'll drive 100 miles to see you get buried when you die. That can be your family or whatever. You better start living. See, I had to stop going with the flow. Things go bad, losing people. My business isn't where I wanted that. My favorite term was, 'It is what it is.' They call that going "through the motions." Going through the motions, just out here existing. Then it comes a time you will either stop making mistakes or start making changes. Start living.

CHAPTER 13

SELF INFLICTED PAIN

A in't nothing like self-inflicted pain. When I was young, I used to hear people say, if you know better, you should show better, and if you knew better, you'd do better. I heard that all my life. Check this out; public disrespect that comes with private apologies is crazy. See, people will embarrass you, humiliate you, go way too far, make you feel less of yourself, and make you feel bad right in front of your family, the crew, the teammates, coworkers, whatever it is is, right in front of everybody. They want to apologize behind closed doors when ain't nobody looking.

If you're remorseful and sorry, apologize publicly and directly. Not with gifts or in an inconspicuous way. Be responsible for your role, take ownership, and sincerely apologize.

Let me give you a very serious self-inflicted wound for men; we've all been there. Something that's just known to get you hurt at all times, and we still do it. Stay out of women's purses. Stay out of their phones. We all got experience with it. I know what you're thinking. I better be able to trust mine. It better not shows right up in my face. I'm going to check mine. Listen. You're not doing anything but hurting yourself.

First of all, it's some financial info in there. You don't need to see that it isn't your business. It may be some pills in there from the doctor. You don't know how to pronounce the name of what they're used for. You all just been together for three to four months; it might be a condom from three or four years ago. Whatever it is, stay out of there. Now you're mad. You're going on and on, and this is the cold part; you're doing all that, and you aren't going anywhere. Ain't got no plans on leaving just a bunch of woofing, self-inflicted pain. Nobody is doing anything to you that you aren't doing to yourself.

Yeah, and in the same breath with that, stop bragging and talking about how many years you've been with a person if you've been a fool the whole time. You know it's over; you've just kept going—self-inflicted pain. Now here goes one for my fellas. I never understood this; you can work day and night. All day, two-three jobs; going hard as you can so you can get yourself emotionally back on your feet. And as soon as you get there – not financially back on your feet; you are working hard to get past things so you can emotionally get back on your feet. As soon as you get there, you go back to the people who talked about you and left you for dead. Why do you do yourself like that? Never forget how they were acting when you were at your lowest. That's self-inflicted pain.

When people do bad things behind your back, sometimes, God will bless you right in their face. Never bite the hand that feeds you and then wonder why you look crazy when you end up starving. See, if you know better, you are going to show better.

You got to pray for people that are going through this. Being stuck in a relationship because of your bills, because you can't afford them, or because you can't take care of them for whatever reason is torture. That's hell on earth, and that's real self-inflicted pain. Because it's either based on your lack of knowledge, your lack of hustle, low self-esteem, or whatever it is, you are stuck behind these bills. But you weren't raised like that, you weren't taught like that, and if you knew better, you would do better.

This is one of the self-inflicted wounds that took me down as a youngster growing up, and I hate to be negative; I'm saying it because I still see it so much today. Why do we do drugs while on probation, drive a car with a suspended license, you're having unprotected sex with multiple sex partners. That's a self-inflicted wound. That is self-inflicted pain. You know damn well what the consequences are. What are the odds of something great happening? None. And you also know that it's a hell of a risk and a chance that you take it, but we do it anyway with no one to blame because they're self-inflicted.

One of the easiest ways to damage yourself or bring pain to your life it's just based on some of the information you're taking in. We're all guilty of it; what we're hearing, letting the wrong people tell us how to do this and what they would have done is how they were raised. Now we are doing something in our life based on some somebody else would've done. Man, let me tell you something... This helped me a lot, and I started using this in my life, which got me to another level.

Sometimes, the best advice you can give is to keep it real and admit you don't know but be willing to go to the experts to find the answer.

Self-inflicted pain, to me, is when you can control something but decide you will do something different. Knowing this certain decision you will make probably ain't good for you, but you will do it anyway.

When you choose to repeatedly do something, knowing it's going to hurt you, that's self-inflicted pain. And since you know better, you should be able to show yourself better. You know, for real.

Check this out. This is married with three kids, a house on a hill, and a great family. You find out it isn't right, but you want to keep going. Ladies, the infatuation and the everyday chase, is just so fun. It's making you so happy. Now you're pregnant. He wants to return to his wife and kid when he finds out. First, you knew better, so you should have done better. That pain was self-inflicted.

Homie, you all ain't been together in a year. The sex didn't get cut off nine months ago. She's no longer accepting your money. She's leaving your messages on read; she isn't even answering your mama anymore. Why are you steadily stalking her page and passing by her house at night? Then you finally see something in the yard, you want to kill her and the man, but writing has been on the wall. You just didn't want to see it. That's self-inflicted. You knew better.

I think the best way to help yourself with self-inflicted pain is to start with healthy decisions. Just literally knowing when to do better. Let's put the elephant in the room right quick. Ladies, this man has bought you three drinks tonight. On the second drink, he is already asking you what you or what y'all fixing to do after this. Now you know where your mind is, what he is trying to do, and exactly what he is trying to establish, but you already know you are not about that and ain't nothing happening, not tonight anyway. By the third drink, you are already giggling and smiling, though. You are laughing and having a good time, and you decide you will leave with him anyway. Still, with no plans of nothing happening and no plans of getting outside of doing what you said you wouldn't, why do you do that?

Now the vibe is messed up. Now the energy is awkward. You're feeling some kind of way. He feels some way and based on his words and actions, and how he might be moving, you could be embarrassed now. It was all self-inflicted. You knew better. Guess what that lead to… On your next date with the next man who is just cordially or casually trying to have a drink with you. They're asking, 'Hey baby can I order your drink? And you're like, "Nah, I don't want no drink. I'm good.'

It has carried over to somebody that didn't have anything to do with it from a self-inflicted wound—the same thing for men. You meet a nice woman. She's good-looking, sophisticated, got a lot going on. You are intimidated. You're so starstruck. All you do is talk about other men. The other guys that you are hanging around. How rich they are, how successful they are, and how great life treats them. And the reason you are going to be good is because you hang out with them every day. The next time you see her, they're on a date. You practically introduced them; you gave her away. If you know better, you are going to show better.

Yeah, you lost a really good one from a self-inflicted wound. You tricked yourself at your own spot. Seriously, that's why I'm jumping into this one. This is a killer. How do two people who can't stand each other got nothing in common? Ain't no way in hell they should be together. How do they end up with multiple kids? Now both of y'all life a disaster from a self-inflicted wound; one of y'all should have made a decision to know better.

I know cats who got plenty of street-savvy. Oh, you're just street smart. You're from the hood. Last month you gambled your car note, and you hit. I'm talking about hitting big. This month here, you've decided to double down. You done lost everything. Missed your rent. Your car is about to go back. You chose gambling over your priority. That's self-inflicted. You know better.

How do you stop self-inflicted pain? By knowing that you had the power or the control of something, you're going to use that not to make a bad decision that you know ain't right for you and that it comes with pain.

This could be my friend, this my family, my loved one. I'm giving them my support. But I know in my heart we will fall out of this money. So, I'm not going to be an investor. I'm not going to give out a loan. Now, I'm looking for nothing back if I decide to do that. Do you know what I'm saying? Because if they are already in the hole with you from years and thousands of dollars, if I give you more thousands, that's the result of a serious self-inflicted wound.

Check this out. If you're moving on, you can't. If you are not going to pay them right, you can't get their services. You can't do the work if they are not going to pay, you know what I'm saying, give you what you deserve, all your money; then you can't do the services.

Why do you keep hanging with people you know are talking about you?

Self-inflicted pain, that's all it is, all of that. You got two DWIs and a breathalyzer in your car. You are still trying to get a ride to the liquor store. You know better than that. You got two cavities, a root canal, and a wisdom tooth that just got pulled. Soon as you leave the dentist and take it out, the first thing you do is smoke a cigarette. On that dry open socket, just excruciating pain, but you knew better. You just did what you wanted to. Out of control, self-inflicted pain.

Always remember this. The first time, shame on you. Then that's for whatever you did; the second time, it will be a shame on me to allow it to happen again. Don't sacrifice your happiness for anybody else. Stop being mad all the time for not getting invited to certain things. You may be getting saved from somebody you don't want to see or something you don't need to see. Do you know what I'm saying? I had to get my own life together. Self-inflicted pain was killing me to the point where I had to start recognizing; you know what? I'm going to start making better decisions before I start letting certain things happen to me.

When you are going through a rough time, the worst thing you can start telling everybody—is sharing it with people you know you don't have any business sharing your business with. They can't wait to tell everybody now you want to blame them, but it's your fault. This the same person that's telling everybody, that's telling you everybody else business, what made you any different, you knew better. That was a self-inflicted wound.

If you just came home from jail with five years of parole left, your ride in the morning time probably shouldn't be your partner who smokes weed in the car all day and who is still hitting licks. I know you miss the atmosphere, you are in love, and you know the whole lifestyle with the homies; you miss it. But you are playing Madden every day in a trap that might not be for you. You know better. You're about to get an out of place case, and you'll have self-inflicted pain. It's people who can't stop reliving tragedies and bad times. Do you know what I'm saying?

Like when I got shot, nobody came to see him when they had a car wreck. You know how they lost everything. People wake up and relive these moments every day—self-inflicted pain. See, for me, if I don't feel welcome or if I feel uncomfortable, I'm grown enough not to go. Start getting used to saying no and dealing with what comes with that, or just keep saying yes and hurting yourself and doing things you don't want to do. I had to learn to hold my tongue and keep certain comments to myself and myself because I know better.

Don't press in on that post; the backlash will be too big for your stress level. But if you do it in a way, now you're reading the comments, and you're hurt—self-inflicted pain. Take control of your actions. Show yourself better because, in your heart, you know better. When you finally get your happiness, that can also be self-inflicted. We out.

CHAPTER 14

PEACEFULLY UNSATISFIED

I'm so grateful for everything I have. My appreciation for what I've been through and what I've been blessed with is unbelievable. But I've noticed when people have been challenged in life. They've been through a lot; as soon as they start to overcome certain circumstances and start getting past certain things that they didn't think they could, the first thing they do is set their mind to be very appreciative and very grateful for all they have, which you should. But just because you're blessed doesn't mean you have to be satisfied.

We often become so grateful and content with what we already have that we don't get to reach our full potential. People will put a ceiling on their growth and never get a chance to see where they were headed or where they had a chance to go. And then look, God will have people around you who can see more potential in you than in yourself. They got more faith in you than you do. You have to recognize that, sometimes as a positive, not a negative.

I've seen people shy away from leadership all the time. I was backing out of big roles, just scared to step up to the plate because it's too much pressure. Now, this doesn't apply to everybody, but pressure can bring the best out of some people. See me. I love when my back gets the ball. I'm a winner. I love to compete. Now, I can accept the loss, and I can do it with grace, but yea, I'm a sore loser because I'm not never comfortable with losing. I can make peace with it, but I'm never satisfied. Peacefully unsatisfied.

I remember when I finally got a chance to buy my first house. I'm talking about excited, elated. Now, this is one of my most grateful things and one of the most appreciative things I've ever been to that's becoming to me. It's one of my goals in life that I finally accomplished; it's one of my first big purchases. Now, based on where I come from and the environment I was raised in, this is huge for me. I thank God every day. But I wasn't there for four months and was already ready for something else. I was already ready for something bigger; what's the next challenge? I couldn't even tell nobody. They probably think he is so ungrateful, but I wasn't. I loved the house. I wouldn't change my route to get it for nothing. I wouldn't change the course I was on to get that place. I just was peacefully unsatisfied. You know, I knew I had worked hard. I'd seen the dedication and effort that I put in. I watched how focused I became. And I realized that I could have anything else I wanted if I worked hard; if I applied myself, even more, I could get anything.

Now it didn't to be right at the moment. I love the place. I'm about to enjoy it, but I still ain't content. I still ain't satisfied. I feel like I still have unlocked potential. What's the worst that can happen? That it doesn't happen. That doesn't stop me from dreaming about it. That doesn't stop me from chasing it or believing I can have it. That's manifesting, peacefully unsatisfied.

CHAPTER 14: PEACEFULLY UNSATISFIED

Now listen, I'm not telling you it's something wrong with being satisfied. I'm not saying that at all. You are supposed to be satisfied with things in your life that you accomplish. Please enjoy your blessings. Please be appreciative and grateful for what you have. That's not what I'm saying. I'm talking about people who set goals, accomplish them, and be on the brink of something even bigger and settled. But it's so much greatness left in them; they have to unlock that potential. It's people who have what it takes inside of them to make others if they just keep going. That's why I say peacefully unsatisfied. Ain't no pressure. You aren't out of control. I'm not losing my mind. I'm grateful. I'm very appreciative, but I want more and am willing to work. I don't mean any harm. I'm blessed, but that doesn't mean I'm satisfied.

I know many people who are satisfied based on their family structure. It could be your upbringing. I heard a preacher say, "you can have pint-sized parents." Do you know what I'm saying? "But your mindset and visions may be the size of a gallon." I had to take that in and try to understand that. Even for me, my parents for sure, and I'm pretty sure my grandparents believed in going to school, graduating, getting a good job, and taking care of your family. That's okay. That's something to be satisfied with based on where they came from. But to get that out of my mind, I had to start dreaming bigger. I had to work hard and surround myself with people who felt it was more to life than that.

I can own my own business. I do have talent. I want to travel the world. I'm appreciative of everything that they taught me. I'm just not satisfied. Peacefully.

Stop waiting on the bus at the airport. Stop looking for miracles to happen in places that they can't. Let that shit sail on—them unrealistic expectations. The answer is to go to work and stop being so satisfied with just doing enough. If you don't want to do more or don't want it, that's your life. You live with that. But stop trying to talk people into that same mind frame because you are satisfied. The dream isn't coming unless you get it. Take the luck and the miracles out of your resume. You must have faith in something and keep going—people are waiting for money to fall out of the sky. And the crazy part about it is they are trying to convince other people to wait with them. Just because you are satisfied with your game plan doesn't mean you need to implement that game into somebody else's dream. You know, you are killing their unlocked potential because you're satisfied.

So, let's go deeper right here. Check it out. There's a big difference between a provider and a husband—between a homemaker and a wife. A provider can bring home the bacon, keep a roof over your head and earn a good living, but he isn't romantic. He's boring. He doesn't nurture, don't uplift, don't pay close attention. Do you know what I'm saying? Same thing with the woman. She can organize the bills well and keep a hot meal on the table daily. All the clothes may be clean and the kids straight. But your sex drive died. You know you don't go to the beauty and the nail salon as often as you used to; you're picking up weight, and your attitude is bad.

So yeah, they could be grateful and appreciative of what you bring to the table. It may be a peaceful environment. But you're barely talking and are far from satisfied in your marriage. You want more.

There are certain jobs, and people you can do some work for will never see your worth. They'll let you work ten years straight without a raise if you let them. Just because you're going through a rough patch and starting from scratch, you're more than grateful for the opportunity and come in peace, but that doesn't mean you need to be satisfied. That isn't your final destination. You got way more chapters in your life to write.

People always ask me, Ke, you love to go hard as you can. You ain't never satisfied. Will you ever be satisfied inside of a relationship? Will you always just want more or something better? I say no, that's not true. I will never be satisfied with the inside of a relationship if somebody let me or me let somebody not give all that we got to get the best out of each other, instead of just having a relationship because it's the most popular thing to do. It's the most traditional thing to do. I'm not going to ever be satisfied with that.

Here's something to be satisfied with. Be satisfied with leaving it all on the field. Be content with never giving up. Be the peace that you gave everything that you had.

See me, one of the biggest investments I ever made was in myself. When I started believing in myself and having more faith in myself, I started seeing different results. Every single day, I count my blessings. I'm grateful. I made peace with many things in my life but being complacent ain't one of them.

I tell you, what if it all ended today? Would you be satisfied with your effort? And that should be in anything you do. Are you satisfied with the part you played if your relationship ends tomorrow? If you get fired from your job today, are you good with your work?

Stop letting people convince you that it's something wrong with you because you want more or better. It's okay right to let somebody else love you. Changing your career path is okay if it isn't working out.

Just because that didn't work out doesn't mean it's over. That doesn't mean you have to be satisfied with making it to that point.

Let me tell you something. The first word or one of the first words that go with satisfied is, I'm tired, I'm good, I'll be alright. No, you won't. Because as long as you have more in you, you will always have that feeling of unfinished business. Do you know what I'm saying? When you lose your confidence and question your ability, you start being cool with mediocre results.

See, I'm passing attitude as long as I get a 70. Barely getting by, but you're satisfied. You went hard as you could, you did enough, and that's what you came up with. I understand if you feel I could've read a little longer; I didn't have an extra hour to study. Now your report card in life got an S on it, satisfactory.

Do you know what's next? The more you don't care, the lazier you will get.

Not giving it your all, not finishing, and quitting early can become a habit. And based on the people that surround you, that might never change. Just because you hang around people who have set their bar low and reached their full potential or made it to where they want to stop doesn't mean that's your cut-off point. Why are you scared to pass people because you think they will be mad at you? Yeah, it's people who stop chasing their dreams. It's people who didn't finish their journey, and they get offended when somebody else wants to finish theirs. Now you are satisfied because they are satisfied. But your work ethic and drive were different. Yeah, you are blessed. Yeah, you're grateful. But you are peacefully unsatisfied.

One of the main things people do when they are satisfied is settle too fast. Stop playing it so safe all the time. People would do the bare minimum in life for a win. Then turn around and expect somebody to do it way out the roof. Your expectations for them are out the roof, but it's not the same for yourself.

Check this out. You watch your favorite teams and want them to die for a win. Getting to the playoffs isn't enough; you want the Super Bowl. Your favorite player scored 50 points, but if he lost, you aren't satisfied; you want to win. But why doesn't it work for you? Why don't you have the same drive and mindset for winning? But you have high expectations for someone you don't know, but you don't put yourself under the same standards. You are satisfied, which leads to this. When you plan a team game, and I'm not talking about sports, I'm talking about your business, your family, your loved one, whatever. Pay close attention to people that just satisfied and happy with individual accolades.

As long as they've won, they're cool. Real leaders celebrate team wins. Stop being at peace with coming in second and third, and at least I finished. Be motivated to come back. Yeah, I lost this one, but I went hard as I could. I'll be ready for the next one because I'm peacefully unsatisfied. The reason why I go so hard is because of myself. I remember being satisfied. I wanted the drugs, to play my game, and pay my bills. I'm good if I can be high, as long as I can be high and enjoy my space in my own house. Nearly ten years went by before I realized I had nothing.

I had none of the things I should have based on the potential I knew was inside of me. The first thing I did was start to eliminate doubt. I stopped praying for money and material thing and started praying for faith and strength and toughness and how to be resilient. I was tired of settling. I'm unsatisfied with my performance in life, and until I get that right, I will be peacefully unsatisfied.

In closing, some of the best traits you can ever have are being grateful, respectful, appreciative, and recognizing your blessings. That's a great thing. But one of the worst things you can do to yourself is not to get the best out of yourself; depriving yourself of the greatness that's in you just because you're lazy, or you gave up or didn't know how to pull it out yourself. Ain't nothing wrong with being satisfied with certain things in your life. But remember this. At the same time, don't ever let somebody judge you or convince you that you are crazy for being unsatisfied. Peacefully. We out.

ABOUT THE AUTHOR

Marcus lakee edwards "Lil Keke \Da Don Lil Keke well known as a southern hip hop pioneer a texas legend and the true architect of the Houston hip hop sound & culture With a career that has stood the test of time & has span over 25 yrs which has resulted to millions of independent sales worldwide Lil Keke is also known as the S.U.C. Captain for his role and his leadership in the legendary hip hop family the "screwed up click" standing along side of Dj screw in the late 90"s His mixtapes and freestyle are a major apart of Texas history and has played a very big role in many of houston's mainstream artist and their rise to fame The father of 3 boys and a pillar in his community. Lil Keke has volunteered managed and coached his own youth football programs In 2014 he was recognized and honored by President Barack Obama with a Lifetime achievement award for his constant efforts in the community. One year later he was given his own day in the city of Houston July 13th 713 day. 713 day is not only a holiday in the city it's also a day of giving back to culture with block parties school supplies for all age students and different health screenings for the community It represents Lil Keke's well known brand " 7thirteen" which is the houston area code , he also extends his brand with a division of it call "Slfmade" which represents his journey his legacy and his ability to substain consistency and longevity in his long career His latest album " LGND" which was released in Feb. 2022 Produced by Justice league Juicy J Mr Lee DJ Chose is another classic in catalog which contains over 50 titles Lil Keke has established his self as legend a true pioneers and a entrepreneur that's now expanding his brand to new partnerships with his own beverage and apparel deals Lil keke the Houston Rap Legend continues to take his platform to icon status

www.ingramcontent.com/pod-product-compliance
Lightning Source LLC
Chambersburg PA
CBHW072013290426
44109CB00018B/2223